Order this book online at www.trafford.com
or email orders@trafford.com

Most Trafford titles are also available at major online book retailers.

Note for Librarians: A cataloguing record for this book is available from Library
and Archives Canada at www.collectionscanada.ca/amicus/index-e.html

Printed in Victoria, BC, Canada.

ISBN: 978-1-4269-0951-1 (sc)

Our mission is to efficiently provide the world's finest, most comprehensive book publishing
service, enabling every author to experience success. To find out how to publish your book,
your way, and have it available worldwide, visit us online at www.trafford.com

Trafford rev. 5/6/2010

www.trafford.com

North America & international
toll-free: 1 888 232 4444 (USA & Canada)
phone: 250 383 6864 • fax: 812 355 4082

FLUSH!

To Holly

Love is the constant we cannot divide, and so we suffer.

With grateful thanks to my editor and friend, Rod McCormick,
without whose guidance and support this book would not be possible.

Poetry
N'
More

ENTER

Somewhere, something incredible is waiting to be known.

Carl Sagan

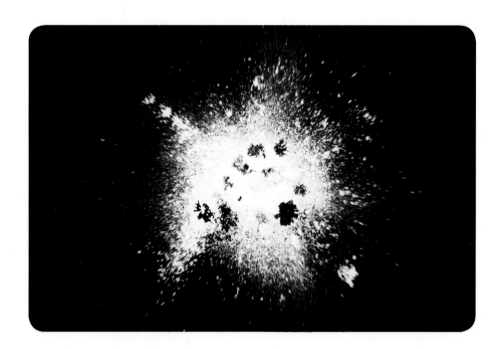

The Big Bang re-occurs as often as necessary to
support the demands of our insistence that illusion is real.

Contents

Love is all there is.

The Beatles

Love is life!
Love is eternal
Love is the only security
Any relationship that does not nurture
Freedom above all else
Is anathema to love.

Crossing Over

Crossing over I felt a breeze
A gentle tempting seducing tease
An invite to become undone
A chance to live as few have done.

Sacrificed my security
My worries.

My desires
My fear!

No more me
Removed & free
Dying is the way to be
Life is but a dream.

Energy is a Process to Love

My own belief is that interlace embodies one idea. It is the same basic premise of cartomancy, of astrology, indeed of all forms of divination: that all things proceed from one substance, and that all things are composed of various embodiments of that one thing—a substance, or energy, or consciousness, whose sentient elements turn and contort themselves in an effort to see the entire pattern of which they are a part. In this view the knots and patterns of interlace represent the complicated whole of creation as the embodiment of one strand of essence.

Bradley W. Schenck

Mother to the Dance

All things reflect a common truth (Love) yet we refuse to assimilate the obvious because the price of truth is life.

It is because of the exclusivity of our commitment to energetic life that truth is the bane of our existence. We are our own enemy.

Due to this limitation the Ancients disguised the truth in metaphor and passed it down within cultural traditions. One such tradition is Gaelic dancing.

An ancient secret is Gaelic dance
Old tradition, truth enhanced
Moving mythology in a trance
Mother truth's sacred glance.

Hidden knowledge in rhythms true
The pyramids—Horus, too
Ancient Egypt's wisdom view
Druidic message channeled through.

Continued...

Form & movement, a poem in dance
Reflecting information to save love's chance
Creative madness, feet entranced
Rise to stillness—all is One.

Ego world is such as this:
Lowest extreme—complex theme
Organized to move in line
All things ordered, fast, so fine!

More control, more alone
Faster! Faster! Find my home
All alone, no one to phone
Turning back—I want my own

Advancing now towards the head
For there I know the eye is wed
Stillness has me so enhanced
I am mother to the dance.

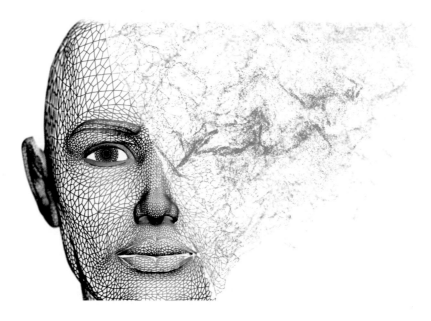

Our immortality is revealed in our constant disappearance.

The Journey

Everything dissolves to love.

Like a harvest
The gathering of one
The knowledge of stillness
Time undone.

To see everything
Gathered into itself
Everything disintegrating into Love
All dissolving into me.

People, places, animals, things
No difference to show
All coming apart
All merging to unity.

To return 'alive'
Full knowing I did not leave
Everything back in place
Now this journey I must face.

Beloved

To the chosen
Love will come like a dull edge
Sharpened to pierce the very heart of evil
It will ask of its beloved
A devotion beyond the body's care
It will not differentiate gender
It will come like a thief but it will not steal
Such a love is not for the weak—
It does not come to the weak
It will require the chosen to cast the spear
Right into the heart of ignorance
By so doing they shall be released
Beyond death into life!
Diving, floating, swirling
Breathlessly into love.

Gathering Home

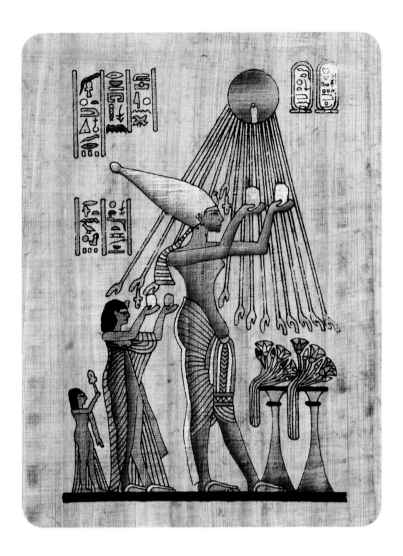

The gathering has begun
Wisdom's shining sun
Dreams of power to come
Dying to be one.

It's the beautiful death
The loneliest quest
The chosen unknown
No one to phone.

Continued…

Beyond ego, beyond pain
Forgiveness!
Fueled by compassion
Driven by knowledge.

Matter transforms in the twilight space
Humility reveals its grace
Its love, its secret
Reach to gather in.

The journey is within
Less is more, gather! Gather!
Carry the harvest home
Watch it die to own.

Infinite Care

Life is Love chasing us home.

To exist in the rhythm of infinite care
Is just a thought from here to there
A shifting gear to ease our fear
The vision to see all things more clear.

A decision to live within the flow:
All things perfect all the time
The flow knows all we need to know
Have to trust and just let go.

The world attacks our wisdom home
Evil has no home to own
Wants us lost on ego's throne
Can only live when we disown.

Continued…

Every person ever born
Is complete in every way
Just as flowers—no doubts delay
It's just this fear that makes us pay.

To exist in the wisdom of infinite care
Requires a leap beyond despair
A sacrifice of fear on the altar of care
And know what gain of which we dare.

Natural Dying

A flower grows, blooms and dies
Billions of others will energize
Constant dying to become
Are they all one or is each undone?

I have watched this constant treat
This noble commanding mystical entreat
Love to observe what flowers know
Feel their message—gentle flow.

Nature flourishes, pregnant with truth
Flowering archetypes in the sun
Each fresh burst a dying run
Returning to the heart of one.

Continued...

Life is nothing but a dream
Anchored in our world of schemes
Nature knows not but to die
Nature knows that life's a lie.

The flowers that die will fertilize
To energize other archetypes
Other teaching tools for fools
Other ways to shout the news.

Flowers & trees, birds & bees
Never demanding, except to be
Man must learn to be this free
Become as nature—there is no fee.

Natural Flow

How do they know the protection
Of letting go
To accept and trust within the flow
Nature has a secret.

All things moving to complete
A natural symphony
Every flower being true
Delighting in its perfect view.

We are all contained within our flower
Little do we know
Only need to change a gear
A mind-switch to become more clear.

Continued…

Our chalice is forever full
Ready to relieve the unquenchable thirst
That pervasive sense of little gained
In spite of islands won and named.

This thundering secret in nature's breast
Seduces us to become undone
Constant pulsing mystical entreats
Salvation begging at our feet.

Nature is our perfect response in time
We believe we are pushing the frontier line
But no, we are really just lost in denial
Defying the art of natural dying.

Moment to Moment

*T*he solution to everything is contained within a moment—any moment!

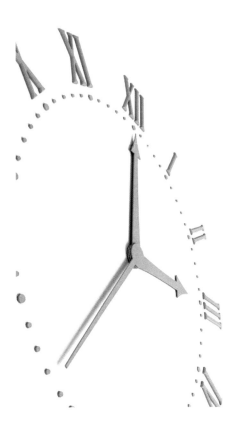

*T*he world is a contraction of wholeness
Heaven is wholeness *ad infinitum*
Time is an illusion that limits the soul
Time allows fear to steal what is whole.

Each moment's replete with the moment to come
Knowing without thinking—the game to be won
The past and the future no longer converge
The world is the oyster—the pearl to be won.

Continued…

This magic exists in the vibrations of matter
Expanding each moment to observe each delight
All senses bared, naked and bright
Exposing fear to die in the light.

Sometimes scared, we panic and run
More often we will build a gun
We speed up our time, afraid what we'll find
Harder to kill a bird that is flying.

But heaven is a moment everlasting and whole
We are all heaven just circling our soul
When we give a moment an expansive mold
We dip from the well of ancestral gold.

Each amplified moment is pregnant with care
Full of the knowledge of what we might dare
Heaven delights when truth has killed fear
Battalions of Angels fly to our care.

Enchantment

Oh, how I love this mortal find
I have moved beyond my mind
I have given up the grind
Only poetry on my mind.

This gentle power
Came to me when love was sour
Told me that I must not cower
That I am destined to know love's power.

Expand the moment, be alive!
Resist temptation to survive
All of time is in the mind
Every moment a portal find.

Many people spend each day
Living tomorrow in yesterday
But, each new moment can't unwind
If there's no one home to find.

Continued…

When you live in moment's true
Matter reveals its secret flow
Your eternal mystic awakes
You will watch the magic brew.

Every day new gifts reveal
Your joy will soar to enchantments anew
Synchronicity will increase
And you will know the power is you.

Warrior

Many are called…

The Warrior on the path
Is always alone
A quiet riot
Breaks new ground
Fearlessly enters no-man's land
Seeking fear—hunting it!
Knows the journey is within
Where humility knows no praise
Where pain is a bandage
Where rejection is the norm
The Warrior's concern is not to be caught unaware
Needs the frontier
The cutting edge

Continued…

Reconciled to equanimity, accepting—powerful!
The Warrior does not want to control
Wants to shape-shift
Wants to die into every moment
To participate in everything & all
Ultimately becoming nothing at all
To be re-born
Naked before the Kingdom.

Lori & Al

A love story

Hey! Little girl, you charm me so
Love your smile, your eyes so blue
Someday I'm going to come back for you
Got to come back 'cause I am you.

Years went by her beauty grew
Always remembered this boy she knew
How his compliments made her smile
Made her feel so specially fine.

Seventeen years old, like a shrine
Blue eyes sparkling like ice on fire
Plenty of apples for her to try
Now forgotten, her boy-man's smile.

Continued....

Tall and dark, big and strong
Macho-wise, he seemed so wrong
She wished she didn't have to stay
Better packages on the way.

Talked of things so pure and wise
The macho died before her eyes
Felt the passion to complete
Felt the urge of ancient beat.

Joined together the heart and soul
No decisions—love is home
True and natural for Al to hold
Complete and natural for Lori to fold.

As a flower wraps around itself
Man and woman—two halves to whole
Melding to perfect what can't be told
To complete the beauty of love that's soul.

Rummaging through the old and new
Found a photo of Al to view
Looked real close, realization grew
Al was that boy she knew.

Merlin knew the ancient truth
Knew that magic was nothing new
Synchronicity insists that dreams come true
When love becomes the master view.

Many lifetimes for fear to slay
Fighting dragons with swords of clay
Now Al and Lori are home to stay
Only little dragons to tease and flay.

Dragonfly

'You also will defend
You also will offend'.

Meditating in a sacred pool I concluded that if all is one, then conversely every one must be all. If every one is all then there is nothing to fear other than fear itself. When we fear we usually respond through defence and by defending we validate and promote violence. If, instead of defending we consciously choose to suffer the consequences of 'non-action' are we not by this decision recognizing that our immortality cannot be subjected to a body? This pro-activity is perhaps the greatest gift that we can bestow on our fellow man—a lonely sacrifice to personal growth by laying a gift on the altar of one's own awareness. I thereby decided that in the future should I be presented with the opportunity to 'non-action' I will answer the call of wisdom and let it be… Just then however, as I was concluding my lofty commitment, I was distracted by a dragonfly who came to test my resolve..

Watched it hover & dip
Hover & dip.

With each dip a flick of its tail
Splashed water onto a lady's hair.

Hover & dip
The lady unaware.

Drew attention for many to see
Hover & dip.

Continued…

The lady's man flicked it away
Came to play with me instead.

Buzzed me repeatedly
Felt its winged breath.

Closer now
A symphony of buzzing threat.

Closer still, attack & recede, attack & recede
In my face! Never touching.

Its challenge bare
I shut my mouth tight to protect.

Buzzed once more and gently touched my cheek
See! See! Its voice declared.

'You also will defend
You also will offend'.

Humpty Dumpty

Humpty Dumpty sat on a wall
Humpty Dumpty had a great fall
All the king's horses and all the king's men
Couldn't put Humpty together again.

In the beginning all was unified
But unity fractioned into multiple forms:
Losing itself in ever increasing complex divisions
Alone, forgetting, fearful—reacting!

Continued…

Dividing—still dividing
Man and woman
One as two
Free will—the protagonists revealed.

Divide & conquer, duality of sin
Split personalities, ego systems
Hate, paranoia, despair
Dividing—still dividing.

When will it stop!
Inventing distractions to race the pain
Reaching a point of diminishing return
No more running—trapped!

Moment of truth:
Only Humpty can put Humpty together again.

The Pony Knows the Way

We ride our wild ponies to the heart of our own darkness
When the pain becomes un-bearable
We may turn back
Or not!

If we refuse, if we defer
Again and again we will wonder
And through our pain we will cry
Why me?

Why this affliction that haunts me
I did nothing but you came and raped my childhood
I was innocent
Why me?

Of course it's you
It's always you
You own your pain
You created it.

Continued…

It follows you like a loyal dog
It belongs to you
It will not go away
Until you choose to love it.

When you love your pain
It transforms to love
Just as a raw material to product
So also pain to love.

There is a world we do not know
A place we need to find
The pony knows the way
Let him loose.

Let him loose
Put the whip away
Let him loose
The pony knows the way.

The Dawning of Reality

To be powerful
Is to maintain the humility
Of subservience.

To launch into non-expectation
Basking in the delightful freedom
Of acceptance.

To reach shore
With the eyes of wonder
As each new environment reveals.

To accept it
Without judgment
Without doubt.

To simply flow in its love
Accepting all as perfect
A perfect possibility.

To become humble in the knowledge
That we are loved beyond imagination
To observe quietly the dawning of reality.

The Student Learns by Daily Increment...

The student learns by daily increment.
The Way is gained by daily loss,
Loss upon loss
Until at last comes rest.

By letting go, it all gets done;
The world is won by those who let it go!
But when you try and try,
The world is then beyond the winning.

- *Tao Te Ching* (Lao Tzu)

Drove away
From the fruits of my labor
The American Dream
Told the kids 'If I stay I'll die!'
The younger cried
The older said he understood.
Drove to the sea.

Lived with strangers who were sad
Drugs and booze
After a year, forced to move
'Where now?' I asked
Love said:

Heed me well
The bills get paid
Find your home
Now, I walk off the beach
To my ocean view
Lunch from the Lobby Gourmet.
They deliver.

Continued…

Sat on my balcony
Dined 'mid crashing waves
What a swell!
A ne'er do well
Tomorrow they may tell me to go to hell.

Thought I could afford two months—
Maybe three?
Entered a magic kingdom
A living poem
Hand in hand
Did not know what held me so
Months became years before the call.

Looking back
I realize the beginning of a relationship
An introduction
The beginning of a new awareness;
A higher love.

Now training to lose
Dying to win
Found to never end
Learning to move and bend
Letting go!
No death to mar this sacred wind
A 'royal flush' that can't but win.

You Is Who You Ain't

Thousands of mythic scenarios
To introduce you to yourself
'Cuz if you ain't who you is
You is who you ain't.

If you ain't who you is
Then you're something else
Something less than you
Something not quite real.

But then, who are you for real?
You are complete
Nothing less, there is no more
You are everything at home.

Jesus said he has weaned us with milk
Because we are incapable of real food,
Did his best with the means he chose:
Taught by example, told us stories, used magic.

Continued...

But after he died we capitulated
Bartered his sacrifice for a golden crown
Missed the point!
We are within, always within—never out.

If we ain't who we is
Then we are not real
If we are not real, we are illusions
'You is who you ain't.'

We exist within these illusions
Accepting their apparent realities
The alternative to stepping outside
Too great a task—too much to risk.

We are as babies peeking out of armor
Trying to be safe & out of sight
But the monster dwells within the shell
Keeping the babies safe in hell.

To become who we are
We must be free to grow
No restrictions designed to control our flow
We must lose our fear.

Screen after screen we must burn free
Climbing the steps of the pyramid
Keeping our focus in violent storms
Trusting 'who we are' when there's nothing to hold onto.

As illusions fall away
We become more & more real
More & more aware that we are still not real
Gaining the sense to know the deal.

When the vibration ache has ceased
We will be released into the nothingness of everything;
The stillness of completeness
Finally, we will be who we is.

Fractured Deities

Male & female—broken, afraid, alone
Relentless desire to bond
To couple, to complete!
Bringing more in to ease the fear
To validate the need, to ease the pain
To justify existence.

In the natural world
Procreation can fulfill its complement
They do not judge or try to control the balancing equation
Humans resist death
We do not respect higher systems
That measure our limitations perfectly.

Continued…

We are as a spreading cancer
To be purged like constipation
There will be no mercy
Our mother earth has lost her milk
She will replenish as we reduce
We have denied her, we have denied ourselves.

We do not accept that we are divine
By our denial we have deprived ourselves
We are unaware of the conspirator;
The beast of darkness
That abides in each & every one
We do not see that which sees through our eyes.

We must return to nature
Hear its chorus of hope
Its endless entreating refrain
To harmonize with her rhythm
To enter her care and have a perfect share
Of endless love to bear.

To become as the birds in the air or the leaves on the trees
To enter unity and gather ourselves up
To stop the leaves from falling
To reverse the driving whip of the beast
To know that we are not balanced for instinct
To accept our limitations.

Each seed must grow its own flower
No more child abuse
No more increasing & multiplying
No more bright eyes & trusting smiles
As we gather them into the furnace
Of the responsibilities we refuse to bear.

No more percolating to wholeness
Over-breeding & associated tensions
Eating our mother alive
We must reduce or be reduced
Each parent must birth alone
The child they once were known.

Continued...

We must tend our garden with awareness
Recognize the beast within
We must understand that life is a process to love
Harness it to pull our plough;
To till our fields of clay
To gardens where children play.

NY Cameo

On the train last night
An evening in the light
Penn Station I was bound
Indian native sounds.

A band was in full swing
Organized trampling Penn
Instruments of wind
Lore from ancient things.

I rose to meet the street
Bitter cold, moving to the beat
Taxis flying around
Pregnant purpose reads the sounds.

I caught her vacant stare
Homeless in despair
Freezing in the night
A lonely troubled sight.

Homeless

I met this gentle man one misty evening while walking in Manhattan.

Said 'I'm hungry, help me please?'
Passed him by just like a breeze
But something in his voice so soft
Told me that I was aloft.

Turned around and said 'How much?'
Saw his eyes of blue so soft
Took him to Kentucky Fried
Watched his face—he could have died.

Continued...

Name was Steve, homeless, alone
Became this way when love grew cold
Everyone from him disowned
When he chose to drink alone.

Only half a family to know
Never belonged, outside the fold
Sexually abused, so confused
Life disowned—love is cold!

Never knew a love defined
Only knew love in decline
Everyone was moving through
Looking for their perfect view.

Went to college, much to share
Knew the philosophic Socratic dare
But none of this replaced the view
That everyone needs someone to care.

The lowly street came into view
At least down here all fit one shoe
Every hour a state of grace
Wondering what will feed disgrace.

Said he wants to begin anew
Forty five and death in view
Wants to build some self-esteem
So depressed, what is real?

Hugged him true but left him blue
I just walked away
Did nothing much to ease his plight
Only left him to the night.

Often I think of Steve so thin
Maybe he died on the street that night
Maybe he was paying for my sins
Maybe now he is fulfilled?

Waiting for the Muse

Borders Books '98
Waiting for the Muse
Coffee, bagel n' cheese
Casual magazine.

Feel you within
A coffee percolator
Choosing its flavor
Will I be worthy?

Is my intention pure
Have I prepared myself
Have I released enough
Have I died enough?

So much that needs to be said
To help rationalize our persistent genocides
To normalize us to some center
To keep us steady.

The keys are within me
Within you
I drink another coffee
And I quietly pray.

Shark!

Divorce time

*W*ent to hire the biggest shark
Learned this lesson from a mark:
If you dance with demons dark
Better find an evil skhrkk!!

Read his story, what a lark!
Might and bite and lots of bark
Tacky celebrity is his tease
Dominic is a Big Mac cheese!

In he came rotund and kind
Thought he knew me?
Centered in the moment's rhyme
Knew how to cast the line.

Said he was like a priest—it's true!
Always playing, such a view
Felt a moment out of time
Enjoying this ancient fiend of mine.

Continued…

Has the measure of what's true
Knows the ladies are centered too
Most of life is quite askew
Can't be blue, fun is true!

Good to swim in Dominic's wake
Feel protected, much at stake
Feeds the shark tight in his keep
Silent, focused, flashing, deep!

Old Farts!

They missed their moments
Because they were unavailable at the time
Now, they look in the mirror and say

'Who the hell are you?'

An illusion changed to quantify the loss
But hark!
A breath still issues forth.

Perro

Sidewalk despair
These beauties came
Accepted my attention
Stayed as long as ought
Maybe they sensed my loneliness
Maybe, without knowing anything
They knew their own perfection—
Don't need to know anything at all?
I need to know everything
So I may become as a dog
This hell we call life!

Whoop-de-doo!!

New Jersey Turnpike. A police officer was shot to death after he stopped a car for a routine check. The perpetrator was a young black man. A few years later, after all appeals were exhausted, the young man was executed. On the day of the execution, the TV cameras focused on the young man's mother who remained at home. I watched as she rolled over and over onto the street in wild despair and utter grief.

Eighteen and wild
Six bullets and the Officer was dead
Death penalty—lethal injection.

Officer's family angry, in pain
Never got to hold his unborn child
Wanted the killer to die slowly.

In prisons solitary he found his soul
But they wanted blood
There was no forgiveness.

Continued…

The young man's father was evil
Beat his wife and kids—out of control
No excuse.

His mother with soft sad eyes
Six other children in prison, victims of rape
She was there for all but the evil was too strong.

Numerous appeals to save her son
Years dragged on
The officer's family more inflamed.

Wanted their pound of flesh, to get even
The mother's reaction through tears of abject desolation:
'Well, Whoop-de-doo!!'

The day finally came
Officer's family waiting in the death room
The big moment!

The young man strapped to a gurney
Would he look them in the eye and apologize
Would they refuse?

Would he die in disgrace
Would they gain relief from looking into his terror-stricken eyes
An eye for an eye.

They waited
And then he quietly said:
'I kneel to no man.'

He was already dead
Beyond fear
The Executioner did his deed.

His Mother, at home, fell to the floor
Ran to the street and rolled and rolled
Out of control with grief.

He died well:
Saw the nature of the beast
And denied its pound of flesh.

He was his mother's son
He will rest in peace
'Whoop-de-doo!'

Holding the Line

In the following poem the man wanted to do the right thing but lacked information. It is not until we learn who we are that we may properly center our actions in the world. In the meantime we will suffer every line of hope just as lines of coke—addicts one and all.

Said he sees the faces every night
64 kills confirmed—proud?
Vietnam vet
Met him doing laundry—just he & I
Showed me how to use the dryer
Discharged on mental disability
Became a biker
Married—3 kids
Grew fat & grey
Sporting a ponytail
Heavy attitude tempered with doubt
Hard to defend the line set down
I asked him about the 64
'They ain't goin' to cause trouble to nobody no more'

Continued...

A boy foraging for cans in a garbage dump
His superior ordered him to shoot the boy
Refused under threat of court-martial
He held fast
A few days later
Three buddies died in an explosion set by the boy
Should he have shot the boy?
He still wonders
Where to hold the line
I asked him if he'd do it all again
Hesitated, then said, 'yes!'
'Why?' I asked
Said there was a military tradition in his family
A place to hold the line
Any excuse to feed the beast
Any excuse to be defined
64 dead boys—madness!

Rasping the Clear

The location of this story is a biker bar somewhere in Pennsylvania.

Aging biker rasping the clear
Drawing attention to ease the pain
Tolerated now—the end is near
A dying warrior lost in fear.

A face like rough-hewn rock
An expert chisel reduced to stock
All the marks of a street dog's mind
Worn like trophies to wars unkind.

Friends of old obliged to care
Pay their dues with funeral flair
Tells him that he looks, real good!
Pathetic gestures like gas on wood.

Continued…

Owner comes by, a heyday friend
Talk trash about the past, of jail time spent
Of Harley's and bitches' and glories' gone
Doesn't want him loud and strong.

Finally, warns him to lower his voice
The customers might hear
Said he didn't mean to offend
The curses just flow like rivers of wind.

Bartender declares 'someone keeps calling to complain
that we're serving a man who has cirrhosis and,
if it continues, she threatens to come and make a scene'
The biker denied the name revealed.

But soon, couldn't contain his anger
Said that she'd caused him refused before
When he got home he'd smack her around
Teach her sense, beat her sound.

Roared off into the night
Six pack secure on his steed of steel
Rasping the quiet for his demons to disappear
A warrior once more too loud to hear.

Fighting Back

Fighting back makes evil sing
Evil has a mighty sting
Forces one to swing to win
Can't abide this evil thing.

Fighting back is what we do
When all our efforts are up the flue
When reason becomes aligned with pain
Reduced we are for control to gain.

Right the wrong is noble and true
Try to change the evil view
But I am also evil's brew
I will play with evil too.

The force that bears is but a test
Choices become the mortal quest
The defining moment within the strife
Is a cross-road to the higher life.

Crime for crime can only digress
There is no crime that has redress
In fighting evil with evil's fare
Prudent evil, sly, aware!

Continued…

The Christian Schism

In the 4ᵗʰ century AD Christianity was dealt a blow from which it has not recovered.

Decisions resound a fatal knell
When made for truth to sell
Once the seed has taken flight
A destructive schism is born to life.

People lost & in despair
No longer knowing the truth that frees
Reduced to fear the vast unknown
Shallow graves of lime & stone.

Knowledge is the key to hope
The way to help us see the Pope
As a man that we could know
Just a business CEO.

Wisdom traditions are all spawned
From the truth of one
Wisdom is the common glue
Tradition just the ethnic flue.

Continued…

People felt this wisdom call
Knew it was for one and all
Built the foundation, fanned the fire
Prepared to receive Lord Satan's ire.

The attack became an empire's fall
The test of truth was live or die
They choose to live, and so, they died
Classic test of truth in time.

Wisdom measured by jaundiced need
Became the measure of intellectual creed
People filled with ego greed
Thinking God was theirs to feed.

This state of guile gave vent to bile
Allowed the ego choose its style
Changing things they deemed not fine
Ego wants the sacred line.

When wisdom becomes a pawn for gain
The house grows high to hold the pain
The pain of justifying an end
With watered down beliefs that bend.

How can we understand this world
By covering up the face of truth
How can we dare to run this race
Without the courage to die with grace?

When chaos reigns
The bump and grind becomes a maze
A maze that tends to grow and grow
Forever confusing the way to go.

It is the tragedy of the West
That those so fine who knew the test
Chose to accommodate & invest
Re-building Rome—new Christian quest.

A mighty kingdom was laid bare
Plunder and pillage was easy fare
The gain was measured—misunderstood!
Christ re-tried and died for good.

Continued…

Many today are lost and blind
Existing within their ego minds
Gave up their right to be divine
By following the dictates of fear in time.

Still they follow to this day
The ego army—swords of steel
Interior styles intellectually signed
Michelangelo—their god designed.

The Angels sang, or so they said
When saints were made in heaven's name
They even claimed that God was theirs
Went with sword to extend the lair.

Incorporated those who knew the truth
Kept them secure within their view
A watchful eye with force to bear
The mystic truth called *mystyschism*.

Penance just a means to gain
God their stock in trade, so feigned
Fear, their tool of woe divine
Ignorance, their finest tool refined.

All things vibrate for love to free
Vibration is God's path to thee
They killed this path to block your view
Austerity became a part of you.

This evil schism thrives today
The maze still grows and rants away
Ignorance replaced by frantic time
Means of control still sublime.

People lost in demon's lair
Shadowed evil watching there
Grabbing shells of fear to feast
Who will stop this whoring beast?

We must equip, begin anew
Face the fear that steals our view
Look it squarely in the eye
Tell it we will run it through!

Continued...

Jesus came, a mystic bold
Metaphysics to break the mortal molds
Re-formed them to the unity mold
Sent them off to save the fold.

The conspirator used the fall of Rome
To drive a wedge where truth was sown
Unity soon became of two
God became removed from you.

Most good thinking after that
Was merely layered fat on fat
Lies to feed the lies before
Massive structures of gold and stone.

This evil schism has had its way
The tragic debt we now must pay
From prisons in time we yearn to be free
No one knowing how to be.

The time has come to hold the line
Strike a blow before we find
The point of no return has chimed
Splashed into a lesser clime.

The secret cost of being divine
Is easy to define:
Offer your life and stand alone
Place your future upon the throne.

Become as humble as a flower
All things perfect within its power
No more shadows dark and bold
Only the wisdom that we own.

Wisdom tells us who we are
Tells us why we are
Tells us we are soul divine:
Wound up god-ness in a time.

Rape of Innocence

This poem is influenced by a documentary that described the plight of children in one of the poorer South American countries. It was aired just prior to the Pope's visit.

Foraging for food in garbage dumps
Living out of cardboard boxes
Disease and pestilence in the air
'Papa, have you shown you care?'

'Suffer the children to come unto me'
For only as children may we enter
Humility is the way to be
Papa set these children free.

Sad excitement in their eyes
Christmas in each load's disguise
Another day staying alive
Dirty Angels & garbage flies.

Continued…

'Increase and multiply'
Contraception—not allowed
Every life—the right to live
Jesus crying in his crib.

Massive citadels of gold and stone
No children to dirty the throne of gold
Ignorance keeps it high & cold
Many don't know that they are owned.

Saint Augustine

St. Augustine was a major player in the Christian schism. During the latter days of the decline of Rome the Christian Church was compromised. The test of truth was bared. Augustine did not rise to the challenge. He and others under his influence sold out for the 'thirty pieces of silver' that subsequently built the Church into a powerhouse.

A man of vision
No peer to test his fear
His truth was not new
Inspired by God and true.

A pagan confused
Converted to Christian faith
With words to save our soul
Told us we are One.

Continued…

In Rome the Christians died
Abominations; sport to please the fed
They died for the spark to flame
Augustus called its name

The Romans thought they'd last
So glorious in the past
Filled with ego dreams
Reduced by all their schemes.

They lost their crown of gold
Went too far and found
That they'd run aground
Monism, the reason found.

He answered their attacks
By writing words that gave
The best of Christian prose
The means to increase the fold.

He blamed the polytheists
Scored a Christian coup
He advanced the cause of Christ
They hungered for his view.

Augustine was supreme
He made theology sing
Said that Rome was wrong
That unity was the song.

Barbarians at the gate
Plunder, pillage & rape
A world for them to make
A thirst for them to slake.

This frantic twist of fate
Gave perfect vent to integrate
The truth of all being one
With the beliefs of the conquering Hun.

Success was his to have
But he let it slip away
He feared the barbarian horde
And changed the truth's accord.

Continued…

They wanted God to be
Apart from you and me
They wanted God to be
A servant at their knee.

Augustine obliged:
He changed the truth of one
Made it two instead
Duality realized!

Duality returned—this status quo still burns
Officially revised, intellectually circumcised
We plunged from being free
To splitting up a tree.

It's a crying shame
The fuel has fed to fire
Augustine, the conspirator's pawn
His face has many names.

He interpreted his own lines
To change what was defined
Used his powers and fame
To politic Christ's name.

Psychology was his bent
A genius heaven sent
He chose to win the prize
By building a compromise.

In spite of all he knew
In spite of sacred view
He was afraid to die
All his truth a lie.

He became the central swing
Christ enslaved to push this thing
Power to control by force of Rome
Orderly chaos, gold and stone.

He gave away Christ's gift
He made a Christian rift
Became an ego-seer
And damned us to our fear.

The Black Guards

Religions are usually well intentioned. Invariably however, they are given overmuch license to presume. This license to presume is automatically endowed because there is no reasonable burden of proof that may be applied to their stock in trade.

The following poem is from the Catholic perspective but should not be singled out unnecessarily; Catholicism is merely a different coloration of a common ignorance.

Ignorance is the inability to know who one is.

If we do not know who we are then we cannot truthfully know how to be. If we do not know how to be then we are guessing. Therein lies our dilemma.

They guard the frozen word
With even hand and stare
They make the truth seem clear
Authority on God's fear.

There is little space to grow
For lives are busily spent
In chasing goals
That increase the daily score.

Continued…

Dogma rarely challenged
No time to deal
With thoughts so in-concrete
Matters so incomplete.

The guards pick up the slack
Theology strongly bound
Dogma without doubt
A devil to give them clout.

They read the ancient words
And believe they're complete
They don't know how they are owned
Don't know the mortal scold.

Sex they live without
Women left out
The strong must lead the weak
Better not be meek!

Else the devil comes
Carts us all to hell
They don't accept how love is honed
That women must be known.

They are a wall of fear
Protecting us from ourselves
They are the dupes of Satan
Swinging his sword of fear.

The Beast of Sin

The beast is within!
The beast is within!
Look within for this beast of sin.

We are children of Thought
Thinking tools
Thrown away when worn & used
Lots of fools to win & lose.

Original thought; the first to dare
At first glance became aware
But the children will not leave the fair
Want to play without a care.

And so, Thought watches
See's the children all askew
Can't tell them what they will not hear
Because the Master has their ear.

Satan is this master's name
Thinking is his master game
We are the creator of this shame
We empower it in our name.

The beast is within!
The beast is within!
Look within for this beast of sin.

Goya

Francisco de Goya was a brilliant artist loved by the ruling authority. But, the Muse had other plans.

Such an artist, perfect line
Goya made their world refined
Served them up an ego plate
How they loved his genius gait.

Allowed them to believe in him
Paid his dues, his Christian fine
Painted all their ego's mind
Paid real well to be confined.

Goya's mind was not for hire
He was meant to serve more fine
Spirit came to confront his plight
Told him he must engage the light.

Continued…

His ego reared, this can't be true!
I truly love the female view
But I am man, a better mind
Females are a lesser kind.

'You will paint what is more true
No more wasteful egos wild
You will paint or you will rue
I will force you to be true.

'You painted horrors that men do
I forced you pleading to show the view
Even madness I did imbue
You were such a narrow shrew.'

Man is conditioned to evil's view
All things measure to help him through
Women have the master view
Goya still is Christian glue.

Patriarchy

Oh, how men have stolen light
Fallen angels in the night
Oh, how men have stolen light
Made this world a dangerous fright.

Thwarted reasoning—might is right
What is real is in the fight
They will force the ego's claim
They will even kill and maim.

Continued…

Men are victims in extreme
Forever lost in ego schemes
Don't even know what runs the show
Empty puppets on the go.

Move them here and move them there
Secure and powerful in the air
They will do what the demon dares
They will jump when the demon stares.

The demon fears the female power
Keeps it down—it must not flower
Makes the world a manly fare
Lots of wars to kill the flower.

These demons control the human mind
Sees the weakness we don't know
Matter is the soul's coarser grind
The demon is not matter confined.

Prado

Went to the Prado, got depressed
So much war and ego quest
Locked in madness for all to see
Art is supposed to set us free.

Goya painting for the best
Dinero building his ego nest
Those who pay are those who'll stay
Goya immortalizes their day.

We must love this art so fine
Goya's art must be divine
But art and dinero draw a fine line
This is the elusive ego fine.

Left the Prado's dark design
Entered the Botanical Gardens—part of me crying
Want my art to be more fine
Want the art of always dying.

Felt the power of instant time
Beauty inflaming my ancient rhyme
Bursting forth to say 'Hola!'
'Hello old friend, I love you so.'

All true art can not be told
All true art is freedom's home
Art is love and love is whole
All true art commands the soul.

Politicians, Democracy & Philosophy

Philosophy is the rational and critical inquiry into basic principles of universal truth. These principles enable a solid foundation for society without which there cannot be stability. Democracy establishes its center around the lowest common denominator which consequently and effectively eliminates truthful inquiry as a mass ideal. And so, democracy is the antithesis of philosophy. Politicians are pawns to the lowest common denominator for if they were not they wouldn't be elected. We must learn the truth of who we are in common so that we may raise the common denominator for the good of all.

Sublimation is the politician's way
Noble philosophy reduced to clay
Building walls to earn his way
Gems of knowledge lost in clay.

Philosophy can not a foot-hold gain
Requires a private disclaim
Democracy is a demon's game
Reduced we are by the mass to fail.

The noble politician is compromised
The common denominator will be his bind
Will be the reason he becomes confined
Step outside—he will be fined.

Continued...

Noble thoughts can not defend
When outside the rampant trend
The trend that builds the material view
In spite of all the constants true.

Listen to the heart of an average man
He will show that he's no fool
He is powerful on his own
No way he'll be a tool.

Observe him when the challenge comes
All alone he will disown
All the truth he defends alone
He will want a validation mold

The politician becomes a tailored clone
Many different suits to own
He will answer ego's phone
He will compromise his soul.

Philosophy will reduce to become
An accommodation for an ego fee
The most powerful feeding at evil's knee
Financial security the power to free.

Better houses, cars & clones
College educations to master defeat
To teach them that they must compete
The world their smorgasbord to feast.

Gain & pain, chase the tail
Advance and live like kings to fail
Life a vicious game to play
Better rocket wins the day.

The politician is a chameleon at play
Knows his future is a compromised delay
Public service in disarray
Extinction is the price to pay.

Politicians don't trust what the Ancients told
If they did—democracy would fold
Philosophy would become the center to hold
Truth would release and become as gold.

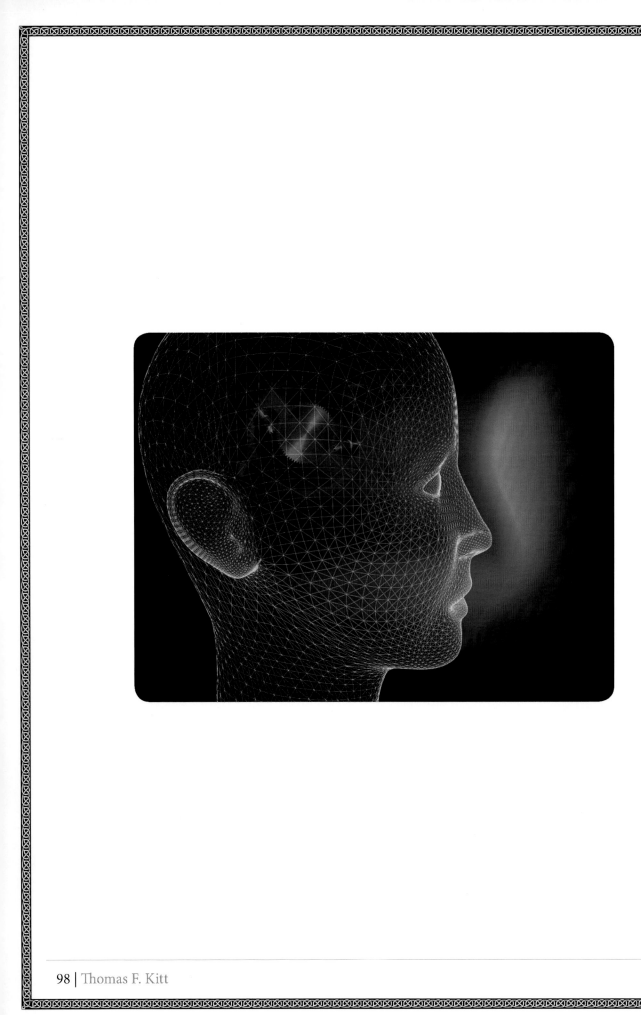

Still

The universe is an illusion.

We are fashioned
For movement, but
Still we are one
Still we are complete
Lest we forget!

Love Knots

All of life
Is Love in confusion
Attempting to equalize
Everything is love
There is nothing else
Nothing to fear
But our own confusion.

The more we center on love the less we separate. Love is who we are but we cannot return to it without first learning the dynamic exchange of our loss. We must learn about our eternal recurrence.

The Big Bang

Understanding the nature of the ongoing Big Bang is the key to the logical understanding of who we are.

The recurrent Big Bang is rooted in eternity.

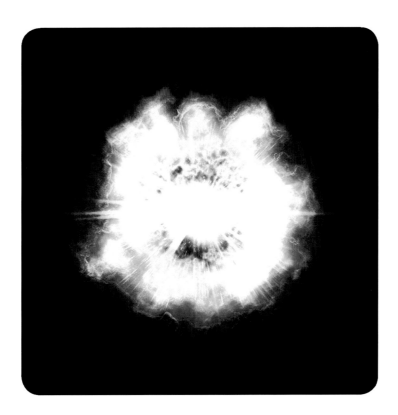

Touch ultimate emptiness...

Touch ultimate emptiness,
Hold steady and still
All things work together.

I have watched them reverting,
And have seen how they flourish
And return again, each to his roots.

Continued…

This, I say, is the stillness:
A retreat to one's roots;
Or better yet, return
To the will of God.

Which is I say, to constancy
The knowledge of constancy
I call enlightenment and say
That not to know it is blindness that works evil.

But when you know
What eternally is so
You have stature
And stature means righteousness.

And righteousness is kingly
And kingliness divine
And divinity is the Way
Which is final.

Then, though you die,
You shall not perish.

From *The Way of Life/Lao Tzu: A New Translation of the Tao Tê Ching*
by R.B. Blakney, page 68. (Published by Mentor Books, 1955)

One 'movie-frame' runs the show.'

One Flippin' Frame!

Everything in the universe has a unique binary code that is a combination from the rapid motion of just one 'frame'.

In movie theatres films are created from multiple frames moving sequentially. Life as we know it comes from one 'frame' flipping fast enough to include all at once.

This is how All is One.

One frame!
One frame!
One inside out
One flippin' frame.

Only One
One frame for all our movies
One inside out
One flippin' frame.

Continued…

Now, now, all is now!
One frame!
One flippin' frame
TIMELESS!

All our movies from one frame
A timeless frame
Everything different
But still the same.

Happening so fast
Our senses reveal
The stories we feel
We believe what seems real.

Lost in our movies
Lost in time
Lost and entwined
In the illusion of time.

One frame!
One frame!
One inside out
One flippin' frame.

When you know the truth behind your movies you will become the director of your own experience—you will command the switch that flips the frame.

Driving the Big Bang

(Excerpt from *Eternal Recurrence... A Step out of Time*)

If the Big Bang was slowed sufficiently it would be seen as just one switch. Imagine that you are in control of this switch and could speed it up or slow it down as you wished. You would notice your observation of the switch changing as the speed increased; it would appear that the faster it moved the more complicated the emergent patterns became (just as a light in the dark). You would also become aware that these patterns were seducing you to enter into experiences that could distract you into forgetting your own information. This is disconcerting because you already know that it is all an illusion being created from a single switch doing nothing more than flipping on and off. There is only one repetitive action, yet you feel a growing seductive force as you increase the throttle (accelerator). In spite of this, and because you remain firmly aware, you do not relinquish your position to any seduction. Instead, you slow the switch down and diffuse all the complicated patterns to an observable movement once again.

Anyone who remembers the truth of the switch has the power to drive it; the power to choose experiences at will without sacrificing power. Each of us is the switch-master, but when we forget who we are the switch takes control. As our acquiescence grows it feeds the fire of destructive negativity that becomes the bursting sores of war, genocide and all other forms of atrocity and discontent everywhere. There is no isolated experience. It is our need to control (denial of who we are) that is the measure of our personal contribution to negativity—the true measure of our spirituality.

Continued...

As we sell our souls to the lesser prize we descend into the common soup thereby coming under the control of a force of such magnitude that through all of time we have not yet even established its existence—such is its power over us. Our position in relation to this hidden force is analogous to what a pebble of sand is to a beach. We are as sparks to this entity's fire and whether a small spark or a large spark the fire owns all. This is our greatest secret never known; the greatest deception since time began.

When we know who we are we will drive our energy to become it.

Science and Cooperation

Science may be summarized as breaking blocks into smaller units in order to use them to build ever more complex structures. In this manner the Industrial Revolution was fueled. Then, in the early 20th century it was discovered that the smallest blocks could no longer be measured because their points of measurement were shifting of their own accord. But, not to worry because we then discovered that if enough of these contrary blocks are strung together we can still control their behavior. Or can we?

The Dancing Particle

Our survival now depends on our ability to cooperate.

We have chased the elementary particle to a level that demands cooperation but we refuse cooperation because we don't trust what we cannot control. And so, we invent increasingly complex playing fields, but no matter how much we move the goalposts we are only biding time for the inevitable changing of the guard. Sooner or later we are going to have to go through this portal. Sooner or later we are going to have to cooperate.

Measure, define and control
Make it belong, make it whole
Nail it down so we can own
Use it to advance the goal.

Technology creates nothing
All is now
We discover and think to own
Just like the Conquistadors of old.

Continued…

What we cannot measure we can't control
Such a dilemma—must control!
The cutting edge of science has found
A particle that seems to dance alone.

How do we explain this wisping whim
Moving around, won't sit still;
A new frontier to nurture fear
Or a virgin birth to become more clear?

Linear complexity, an idiot's delight
This dancing thing just wants to play
Pied Piper piping away
Must turn back or crash and pay!

What is this thing our science can't hold
This messenger entreating us to unfold
A portal, a doorway to a brand new day
A higher rung to see the Way.

The difference between Newtonian and Quantum Physics is that the common laws of physics
begin to deteriorate on small scales. The reason that quantum physics needs complex math
to explain the behaviors and properties of small particles is that the world of these subatomic
particles is a very bizarre one, filled with quantum probabilities and organized chaos. For example,
the exact position and velocity of an electron is very hard to find because attempts to "see" it
involve bouncing other particles off of it. By doing this, you've just changed the electron's velocity,
so your data is useless. What quantum physics does is give us the statistical probability of the
electron's location at any one moment.

- Jim Tucek

I think I can safely say that nobody understands quantum mechanics.

- Richard P. Feynman

Will o' the Wisp!

Dearest Will, please sit still
I want to know your every thrill
Every knowing wisping whim
Dearest Will, please sit still.

Want to keep you in my sight
Close my dear, do not fear
I only want to be more clear
About the reason you are here.

Every time I search for you
I feel you see me through and through;
Looking at my fear-bound mind
As if I am a curious find.

Maybe Will you think of me
As flotsam in the open sea
Quite removed from all that's free
Afraid to release to one with thee.

But Will, if for a moment you would sit still
We could be the best of friends
I would not fear your wisping whims
If I could but see your wings.

We humans must control you see
Otherwise we can't be free
So Will, please don't flee!
Need to have you at my knee.

Siege

The level of cooperation between one object and another will determine the severity of a collision.

The biggest mistake in human thinking is the belief that we are evolving from a singular Big Bang. Our future is powered by this idea and because it is a 'central failure' all is thereby off-balance and subject ultimately to collapse.

. . . .

The 'big bang' re-occurs as often as necessary to support the
demands of our insistence that illusion is real.

. . . .

The ultimate challenge is now upon us and, unless we can re-adjust our center from a single bang to a recurrent bang theory we will be unable to gain the level of cooperation necessary to achieve the involvement that will set us on our true course. The die is cast but we can still change the outcome simply by changing direction. It's personal! We have come up against a solid door that is dispersing our momentum in all directions - we are crashing! To a new beginning – choose well.

Ref. *Eternal Recurrence …A Step Out of Time* by Tom Kitt.

Continued….

The Siege of TUNIS.

Armies massing, pounding roar
Tricks and guile to fool the door
Finest minds combined to schew
To find a chink to scuttle through.

On and on this siege will last
The final outpost of a single blast
But never will they move on through
Because the price is wisdom's view.

They will squirm and steal and screw
All that's required to power them through
Nothing sacred, feast and tear
Spill the blood of those who scare.

Seeding gardens of minds
Training them with fear control
Genetic clones & fascist thrones
Who will cooperate before all disowned?

This saving door will not be moved
Cannot ever be abused
Not until they are released
Will they enter to view the beast.

Conclusion:

We have ridden the 'single bang' steadily to this irrevocable door. Our current center can no longer hold, we will not back up nor will we reduce momentum. We can't go forward and we won't go back and so we are dispersing into even more finite particles that we chase to control with a tool called quanta. But, there is no way around this door for it will not be moved by physical force, complex intellect or guile. It will be opened with the gentleness of a feather's breeze by those who have achieved the courage to shift their center of knowledge.

The future depends on our ability to understand the difference
between who we are and who we thing we are.

Who Really Believes...

The eternal Positive is Love.

Who really believes
The paradox of Positive existing without negative
That Positive is constant in all things;
Equally complete in the smallest grain of sand
As the most advanced intellectual process.

Who really believes
That the increasingly complex negatives we attach
Are constantly shedding like water off a duck's back.

Who really believes
That even though negative cannot exist alone
It is nevertheless the cause of creation
Who can possibly understand that because this is so
Everything in the universe is necessarily illusion.

Who really believes
That without negative the Positive has no reference to itself
That this independence is the difference between power & energy.

Continued...

Who really believes
That all things are illusion
Brought to form by negative attachment;
If negative is removed
Each & all becomes what it already is: infinite.

Who really believes
That we are all miracles waiting to happen
If we just get out of our own way.

A Matter of Time

Matter cannot exist without movement and movement cannot exist without time.

Time is a function of matter
A dysfunction to shatter
Time can not be
When matter is free.

Matter flowing free!
How can this be
No more time
No more dying.

When we depart, life has no time
All exist complete and fine
No definitions by body defined
All complete in infinite rhyme.

Continued…

Time is a function of matter
A dysfunction to shatter
To live in the now
No more furrows to plough.

So stay in the moment
For it's there you will find
That matter must flow
When Love runs the show.

Love is the constant state of all things.

A Devil to Heal Our Shame

The archetype of humanity is completeness (Love).

Few, it seems, are aware that we are controlled to a point away from completeness by a force that we ourselves create.

As we define ourselves in energy we fall from completeness and empower ignorance.

This ignorance concentrates to a unity that battles to maintain its own identity—its own life.

The pain it causes is our means of recovery.

As we continue to deny who we are we empower this force thus the level of pain increases to maintain our possibility.

Our completeness cannot diminish and so there is no choice but to chase ourselves into recovery.

Before we may begin to recover from this debacle we must become aware of how our table is set.

Continued…

Summary:
The accumulation of our denial of who we are is a force of such magnitude that individually we are as a spark to its fire or as a pebble to its beach. Its tragic necessity controls everything and creates all forms of discontent everywhere. Its tour de force cannot abate until we stop empowering it—it is the complement of our ignorance after all and therefore cannot change until we become aware.

Nothing can exist alone
Every life is dependent
Or, so says genius Albert.

Without this dependency we don't know who we are.
Unaware that we are immortal
We are driven to something less.

We give our power to less
A lessening to invest
A force to serve our quest.

We give our power away
To a force that grows as one
A devil to heal our shame.

We give our power to loss
A soldier with a gun
A boy to be undone.

Older now I'm blind
Wife and I are fine
Old age dreams in line.

Children coming by
Grandchildren too
Baked an apple pie.

Nothing can exist alone
Built my life on you
My hopes are found in you.

Continued…

An island in a stream
Other islands near
Ports to fill our steam.

And the world goes raging by
Wars, dissent and pain
Always, always, in every age the same.

But you can't defeat me at my own game
I am not to blame
I have nothing to be ashamed.

Nothing can exist alone
Every life is dependent
Or, so says genius Albert.

Without this dependency we don't know who we are:
Unaware that we are immortal
We are driven to something less.

We give our power to less
A lessening to invest
A force to serve our quest.

We give our power away
To a force that grows as one
A devil to heal our shame.

Movement is Hell!

We are one, but then we move and all hell breaks loose.

We are products of movement
Movement is hell!
Enter the demon to make us well.

Beware!

When we come to energy we separate to become like the isolated units in a common soup; a soup that has control over all that is the sum of its parts.

If you steep yourself in acid
You're going to be burned and assimilated
This is the way of acid
Acid is acid—it doesn't know any better.

If you steep yourself in energy
You're going to be burned and assimilated
This is the way of energy
Energy is energy—it doesn't know any better.

Rust Never Sleeps

In the following poem the word 'rust' is a metaphor to describe our powerlessness in the face of the watchdog we have created to protect our ignorance.

Rust is a reality that wraps around
To define in terms of conquered ground
Like a serpent with venom kills and devours
Rust will not sleep—takes the tower!

'A camel will walk through a needle's eye
Before a rich man will learn to live to die'
The power of living in the prestige of name
Makes him think that life's his game.

The rust clings tight, knows not to sleep
Covers and grows—fortunes to reap
Power and fame will expand and explain
That man is the center of all that is gained.

Illusions ferment in reality's name
Plants a disease in the children disclaimed
They will cry in limos that fly
The parents will try to give them the sky.

Continued…

Rust cannot love, all realities lie
So many influences, powerful—destroy!
Like the Nazis that guarded the Hitler dream
Validation can be a fascist theme.

The ones being born are the fuel for dreams
Anarchy & fascism are in all our schemes
The Holocaust was a bursting seam
Gaia's patchwork through the Jewish scream.

The rusting realities that obscure our view
Are a conspiracy to stop us shining through
The Reality that exists when truth is won
Makes realities change to become all as One.

The killing of rust is a difficult dream
Sometimes requires an innocent scream
A sacrifice of pain to establish a cure
To return to a place all bright and pure.

Child so lovely, I see my face
Hidden in your rust's disgrace
I really want to change your view
Show you the incredible reality that's you.

This world is a place on the edge of Love
A precipice designed by an evil shove
Love locked in matter's fright
Divide and conquer—empire's might.

Cycle of Shame

Humanity is a recycle round 'n round, dancing for the watchdog we dare not name. Who will learn this watcher's game, who will accept we are the same, who will call this fiend by name?

A constant recycle going around
Keep them coming!
Don't even ask
Why so few reveal the mask
And those so few so quickly claimed
To a higher cycle but still the same
Round n' round
No one leaves this game
So says the master of our shame.

INTRUSION

Every human being is less than they actually are and even should they realize who they are; they are still less than they are in reality. The only difference being that they would know it.

When people know who they are they will seek to become it. Thus, the world will heal.

All who do not know who they are become fragmented into different levels of who they are not.

Fragmentation spirals out like a pyramid.

The following poems describe lower levels of the pyramid.

Finger of Blame

When deferment's complement becomes quite full
The mortal man will feel its spell
Like an egg being heated to a boil
Cracks will start to break the shell.

This is our hell to mend
Some crimes committed one can't defend
Angrily they may point to you
But you may simply not have a clue.

Observes a weakness grid it seems
It will maximize its need
It will enter, steal the cheese
Spring the trap, gotcha, freeze!

Under the present state of thinking
Many are open to be absorbed
We give ignorance the means to thrive
Fear keeps it alive.

Fear removes us from truth;
Points of view we accept as real
Are setting us up for a steal
Lost highways to hell on wheels.

Affliction

Psychological and sexual abuse
Violations of divine privilege
Forces the child to acquiesce
Foreclosure, a vicious takeover effect.

'I locked my lovely soul away
I will keep it safe with me
I will protect my soul this way
I will let it out to play.

'I became a master-mind
Lots of friends of my own kind
They would come when I was blue
They would fight to help me through.

The world kept coming, would not stop
I kept crying in my cot
Soon, my friends told me to stop!
No more friends to mop my slop.

Continued…

I reached out to claim my crown
My fear rising so profound
You felt threatened, forced the round
Obsessions and addictions tied me down.

They continued to perform
Very brilliant, no restrictive form
Evil is energy that steals our time
Has no body or soul to mind.

Tragic child louder now!
Sophist rising above the storm
'Incongruous that this child of mine
Can not be raised by my own kind.

'I will teach it to be mine
I will show it that I am kind
I will make it grow my mind
I am Satan to my kind.

'But, still this child keeps me awake
Always crying—it will not take
I intellectualize, rationalize, justify my kind
But still can't stop this soulful whine.'

Should you leave this child will grow
To finally forcefully come to know
That you have stolen its heart & soul
You are the thief that all should know.

Off the Edge

When man has wasted time
He wastes the gift he had to grow
He becomes the waste he chose to be
He is the one who chose the way.

The waste becomes the demon spawn
He is no longer man or beast
For beasts are souls in restful pose;
A time to teach without being told.

Continued…

The wasteful man has lost the right
To enter life in human form
He is no longer in the game
His only game is others' trials.

He watches for an open space
A place to find a little hope
A place to live as he once knew
To waste the life that allows the hew.

The life is harried from all sides
Everyone must free his mind
Try to think above the storm
Watch the children at their play.

The rend becomes the demon gate
An entry point to steal the show
The life will gladly give the stage
To demon sages smart as hell.

The life will languish in this play
Will give the demon room to flay
The demon has the means to win
Because he's smart & full of sin.

The life may grow to detest itself
As all around the evil grows
It watches helpless as a child
As fingers point in loathsome way.

The demon is not there to see
The pain is left for the life to bear
It does not know what caused the pain
It only knows that it was there.

To find your soul you must evict
The loathsome beast that lingers there
Understanding is the key to resolution
To making truth the power to be.

The Now People

The Now people wait!
Wait to attack the weakest point
To gain a foothold
A soul disowned.

A baby born to live in hell
No affection, no love, only knows strife
Maybe this baby is a girl
Maybe, her father is not healthy.

He vents his pain on those he has gained
Sexual abuse, violations of divine privilege
He is angry!
Wants satisfaction, his pound of flesh.

The girl grows up violated & stained
Knows she is strange, alone
Frantic, a little deranged
The Now people come to ease the pain.

Continued…

She finds the means to live
The Now people give & give
In her innocence she accepts all
No choice but to live.

She found a way—a secret way
A secret that none shall discover
But, life demand a normal flow
Must protect these friends so none will know.

'This world's a smorgasbord of fools
No one guessing the friends I own
I can send my best to find
Whatever normality I wish to clone.

'But, the demands never stop
Always changing around each bend
On & on I must defend
Giving my friends the reins to tend.

'More & more I became reduced
My friends in charge have me seduced
I have tried to regain control
But, my friends now claim for all to own.

'Became addicted!
My friends in control
Taking their turns to answer the phone
Sending who will best control.'

Once invested to life
The Now people are very real
Their cling to life like an angel to home
They want to steal what they have lost to own.

They are the refuse of negativity
A vast complement lying in the shadows
Timeless, watching like vultures
A window of opportunity to reveal.

Requiem

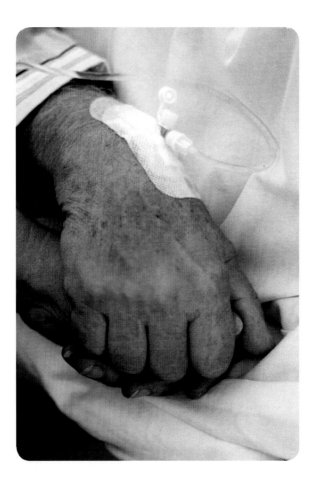

Lying in this terminal bed
Death is circling.

What a price for clarity
Wish I had this sanity before.

So much that I would do
Without confusion or a single doubt.

I would give all that I have
Nothing would I own.

All transient features
In an evolving landscape.

Continued…

I would be as an actor in a play
A symphony on display.

I would watch the scenes go by
Nothing I would delay.

But here now as I die
Revelations dancing in my head.

I realize sadly that now I'm well
Only because I leave this hell.

Destined to Heal

We are destined to heal but in order to do so we must stop damaging.

We are complete
Destined to heal
It is the Way.

As we damage we heal
As we damage we heal
As we damage we heal.

Not a choice; healing is natural:
Stop damaging!
And healing will complete.

We are complete
Destined to heal
It is the Way.

Rhythmic Breeze

Listen quietly and you might find
A special movement, an active find
An intelligent vibration that dances in matter
Available to all beyond the chatter.

Everyone with a story
Each in a world of their own
Hold in tight those things that bite
Release what appears to measure right.

A commercial world of body-fare
Must protect and not declare
All those things that killed love's flair
Must have product for the fair.

Continued…

Many different things to gain
The world has much to build repair
Developing skills and ego fare
Brand new me without a care.

Met a girl who loved my view
All my stuff, my future true
She held stuff that she loved too
Now we have an ocean view.

All things material is a ball in play
All vibrating its special way
Rocks & trees & birds & bees
Rock-a-bye baby, rhythmic breeze.

The mind has many balls in play
A vast array let loose to dance
Intellect measures the juggler's stance
New worlds created—endless trance.

Crashing, bashing—do you mind?
You upset my special wind
I will defend how I'm defined
Maintain the balance of all that's mine.

The big, the small, the rich, the poor
All just swinging a wider door
Hinge gets broken—no more door
This broken door will swing no more.

The world is a ball in play
Gaia working for balance to hold
But, this too, a wave building to scold
Many worlds crash and fold.

Tranquil is the soul at home
No disturbance, no one to phone
All dissolved from matters hold
No more vibration to make us bold.

Quiet Perfections

When the world comes bearing down trust in quiet perfections.

The magic of life
Is revealed through quiet perfections.

Sitting out my window
between worlds.

Watching birds on the balcony
Listening to the ocean.

Ironing, vacuuming, dusting
Cooking, watering the plants.

Collusion with everything
A private discourse with world's within.

Becoming a participant
Through obedience to quiet perfections.

Hearth

*S*itting quietly I ponder
The knowledge that I own
Demons come breathing fire.

I try to ignore them
I am on my journey home
To sit by the hearth.

To watch the turf fire burning
In my cottage of straw and stone
My sacred home, my whitewashed throne.

A cathedral to house the hearth
That burns the demons' hold
There I must abide.

There I must abide—as a child
Naked before the monster's eyes
Guileless and wise.

Butterfly

Butterfly, butterfly
Black on wings of night
Thought filled rocks of light
The angel of death alights.

Butterfly, butterfly
Come and pray tonight
Come to ease my fright
The angel of death alights.

Butterfly, butterfly
I will shed my wings for thee
I will die to be set free
The angel of death alights.

Butterfly, butterfly
I have become your darkened flight
On wings of aged light
The angel of death delights.

Wings to Fly

This painful need to complete into something
To become attached
To be defined & valid
To be finally safe.

To extinguish this fire
This fear
Like pieces of you & pieces of me
Fragmented into all.

Want to give up!
To die into the humility of acceptance
Submitting & melting
Dying!

To be reborn into the act of simply saying
'Thank you for this precious moment'
Releasing it to a new wonder
Giving it wings to fly.

Breathless!

Trusting its knowledge
Its perfect skill
Its creative will
Its beguiling simplicity
Releasing expectation to its care
Pressuring nothing—
Breathless!
Breathless in love awareness
Its challenge
Its demanding patience
Its humbling death.

Bondage

Expect nothing
But the opportunity to embrace your own freedom
Through the freedom of others.

Expect nothing
Other than the promise
That you will be tested within this bondage.

Expect nothing other than this
For it is within this bondage
The giant of freedom sleeps.

Become the one to choose
Choose the chosen one
Many are called…

Release into a spaciousness
Such as points converging
To explode into nothing.

To become the air for others to breathe
The life for things to grow
The one we all must know.

Bliss!

When we learn who we are we will know the perfection of all things and therein find our bliss.

Follow your bliss
Heavenly bliss!
Like a shadow alone
Pulsing home.

The pain of loss
Unremembered loss
Mother and child
Wanting to hold.

To sense without knowing
This pervasive completeness
Sadness…
Close to madness.

Who can define
A soul that is dying
Lost in confusion
The world's an illusion.

Follow your bliss
The pain will insist
Will batter you blind
Love to unwind.

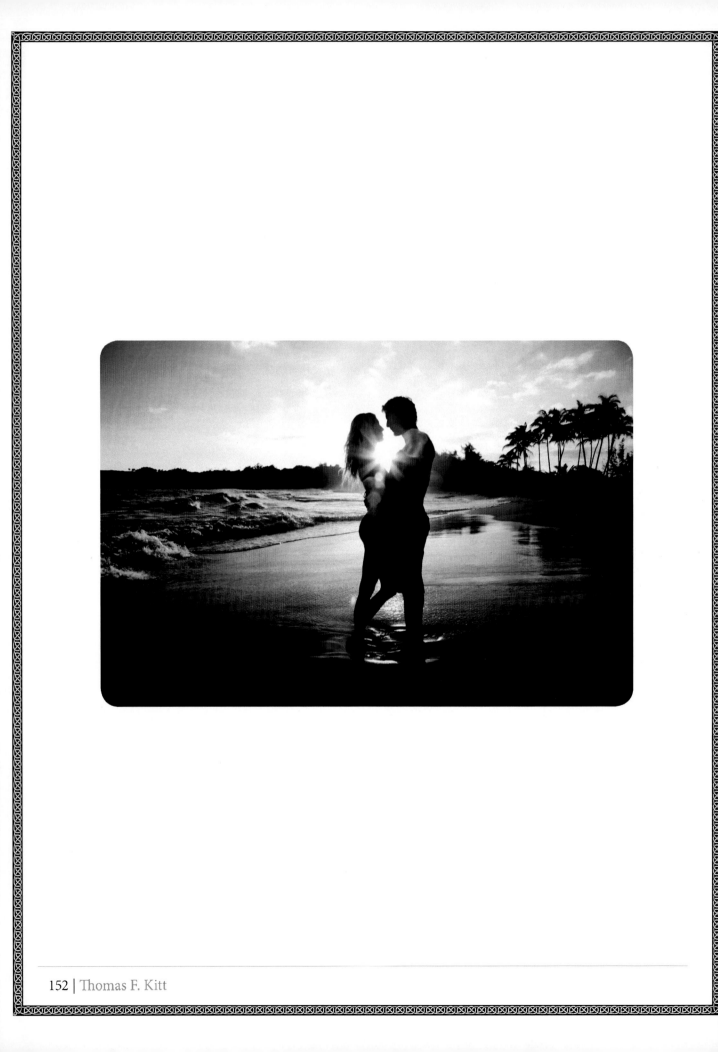

Lover

Lover, lover, you unfold
Like my precious ancient home
I am shadow, oh so bold
Lover, lover, you are old.

Young Women

Young women are truth inspired
Beautiful! To be desired
They primp and preen
Love to have their beauty seen.

They feign that they are most reserved
No coy moment left un-served
Just like feathers in the air
Going away—yet always there.

She makes her move when she feels sure
That he has felt the primal lure
That he will answer her mating call
Provide her with the means to fall.

When the love had found its mark
She may feel somewhat apart
May sense that love was meant for more
Than passion in its primal roar.

Sex is pleasure in excess
A toy for joy to vent its will
But as it is used it becomes confused
If love is not the primary fuse.

The young woman knows the balance point
She has the center in her sight
Wants to reach the highest note
Knows that love is sex's point.

A Face of Love

I was sitting in my back yard when a tiny bird flew into my hair. I dared not move. Later I learned a lesson about equanimity.

All Loves' faces must disappear
Reappear to disappear
Endless faces chasing clear
All Loves' faces must disappear.

Like a bird in my hair
A startling scare
A teacher's dare
A death to share.

She knows the truth of human life
Intuition chilling the dampened air
Living fragile in its care
She watches how it sets the snare.

They open like flowers in the sun
But man is not a flowering run
Each must live to become as one
One is not a flower undone.

Continued…

They come with gifts to tempt
She takes the tease and sees the shift
Sees their bartered light to own
But still she walks her path alone.

They cannot gift what's already owned
For her no bartered security zone
She lives this lonely poem
She knows the art of coming home.

An Angel blurring clear
Clarity breathing in her ear
Whispering sweet nothings she wants to hear
Nothing is everything made clear.

Letting go!
Each hello a fond goodbye
A timeless moment getting high
A river knowing it can't lie.

Like honeyed thorns
Holly in my hair
I want her to know my hello is goodbye
A shooting star to light the sky.

I want her to know
A surfing epiphany on mountains high
A bird of freedom for us to fly
On wings that know that life's a lie.

All Loves' faces must disappear
Reappear to disappear
Endless faces chasing clear
All Loves' faces must disappear.

100% Brand New

If we share some time
I want your secret child
I want you deep & wild
I want to love you blind.

I am learning what to do
In order to be with you
I am learning to be with me
In order to be with thee.

A moment is all I dare
No past or future care
I want to be here now
I want to free the plough.

My horses running wild
Running, running child
Entering the flow
Of places deep & wild.

Continued…

None other will I know
Only a moment's flow
I want to dance with you
One hundred percent brand new

So come and go at will
I don't want to know your sin
How you get your thrill
How you fill your till.

I already know your name
Don't want your karmic shoe
I only want you true
One hundred percent brand new.

If we share some time
No future I need of you
No past to enter fear
Nothing to pass my ear.

Nothing left to say
A pregnant stillness bared
For stillness is our dare
To be as children share.

And when you walk away
I will know you cannot stay
I don't need to know the why
It is your shoe to try.

So if we share some time
Commit to love me blind
Become to one to view
One hundred percent brand new.

Desire

All desire is a measure of loss.

Bright shiny innocence
Fuel of desire
World of fire
Burning, burning, fire.

Sensual, sensual
All is fire
Fuel of desire
Burning, burning, fire.

To enter the flower
Her burning power
World of fire
Burning, burning fire.

Earth Woman

Told me that she loved to grow
Organic farmer, natural, weeds to know
Earthiness her daily due
She is Love in nature's view.

Told me she was free to know
She choose me but I was slow
Couldn't expect this Angel to know
That I gave up long ago.

Met her as we went to shower
Male and female in one tower
She was bleeding did not cower
Bade me wash her in the shower.

Washed her gently
Knew she had exposed the flower
Felt honored to be in her power
Fragile trust to serve the flower.

Continued…

Overwhelmed, I left her—could not stay
Felt unworthy to serve this way
I am man—conditioned
She is natural, the earth is her way.

Breakfast came and she was there
Quietly ignored me—seemed unaware
Said 'I wish to say goodbye'
Hugged me gently, went her way.

Woman's Way

The influence of rhythm
Is found to be
A balance point
A magnetic vibration.

Watch the movement of a woman
In easy rhythm, side to side
See her skin elucidate
The man's desire to be divine.

See her promise come to life
The way of wisdom is revealed
The harmonious chord makes man alert
To memories dormant sleeplessness.

To be a gift to man's desire
To shed the cobwebs of the past
To make him sense his ancient rhyme
To give him cause to stop awhile.

Connecting exquisite chords with grace
She moves in harmony with his soul
Tempting him to know himself
To be enchanted by the joy.

The scene has changed
The shade has come
The magic done
Portal gone!

Continued…

Fallen Angels you have become
To grasp at security is the plea
The best you do is waste your time
In open doors to precious truth.

But the magnet has no care for doors
It only knows that you are fair
The dance of life will take your hand
Spin you around to see the Way.

You are love in disguise
A wonder to behold
A wealth of potent good
One indivisible by one.

Creature of Light

I observed this magical being drawing the attentions of men at a clothing-optional resort.

Does not allow intrusion of her world
She does the intruding
She is wise.

She is in command—in demand
Knows her power, how to use it
Knows to allow them to believe.

That they are stealing
They cannot steal what she freely gives
She is a creature of light.

She sees their limitations
Sees their light
Swims in their light.

Makes them feel good
Said she was born only this very morning
She is a creature of light.

She is now
Always now!
She is aware.

Timeless
Without fear
She is a creature of light.

Continued...

Wise & wonderful
Like an animal
But no, not like an animal.

Said she was Jesus this morning
I knew this was true
(Now you are calling me a fruitcake too—Hah!!)

She is a creature of light
She is God
And she knows it.

Until Death Do Us Part...

We are projections of a singular whole
We defend the images we chose to own
And so, a demon is born to rule
This demon lives through the images alone.

The ring is a representation of our highest purpose: the unification of opposites to a singular crystal clarity—the joining of two to become one.

Whereas the design of the wedding ring is well founded in truth it should be noted that it relates to an inclusive environment and not to a singular couple. The separation into distinct couplets without awareness of the higher objective limits the possibility of achieving the higher state of unity. This is not an arbitrary condition.

Until death do us part…
Fear steals the heart, rips it apart
Too much license for love to depart
In death, love fills the heart.

This kind of defeat is a bartered retreat
Ivory towers to defend most discreet
Traditions abound that feed this deceit
Love forced to grovel at the conspirator's feet.

Until death do us part
An offence to the heart
Prison cells set apart, numbered in line
In death, love fills the heart.

Love is reality—not a containment
Not a trapping to be bartered and tamed
Love is the completion of all we can be
Love will reward if it is made free.

Continued…

Until death do us part...
A dart to the heart
Restricts the flow for flowers to grow
In death, love fills the heart.

This universe is a moving feast
Always replenishing—this mortal beast
Never a moment that is the same
Much may be similar but is never again.

Until death do us part...
Blocks the flow for wisdom to grow
Limits the freedom that love must know
In death, love fills the heart.

Stop a stream—kill its dream
No more perfection bursting to reveal
That death is the reason the world comes alive:
Constant death is a birthing wheel.

Until death do us part...
This control must come apart
A stake through the heart
In death, love fills the heart.

Containing love is the root of disease
Feeds on traditions that socially please
Define and control, refine and seek gold
Love chokes on this need to own.

Until death do us part...
An evil design to confuse what is real
Death is occurring as instants reveal
Death to the ego releases love's stream.

We are projections of a singular whole
We defend the images we chose to own
And so, a demon is born to rule
This demon lives through the images alone.

Engaged

Freedom & love are synonymous. Therefore, anything that tends to contain love is to be examined as to true purpose. We must consider why it is we want to contain love by forming a structure around it. We must consider why we have created a cage called 'marriage' to contain the sweet bird of truth.

To build a life together
Reaching for some imagined utopia
'Good enough for now!
Keeps me occupied
Don't really want to think about it seriously
A carrot in front of my nose
I don't know what to be
No one told me
So, I'll run & run
And when I feel more sure
Maybe then I'll know how to be
Why is it so hard to face this pain
Why do I sell myself for a useless promise
Why do I need to believe in this promise so much
Who am I?
What am I doing?
Running!
Running!
Running!
Away from what?
To become what?
I know nothing only that I'm lonely & scared
And I want to escape somewhere.'

Dilemma

Youthful light shining bright
Locked in matter's shocking fright
So many ways to barter light
Will they fear too much to fight?

Everything is attacking love
Traditions, pressure to marry, family security
So seductive to step in line
Everyone happy—prisons in time.

Will sex lose sight of loves' command
Will they hide behind their kids, seduced by fear
Safe and secure in Satan's mall
Another one coming in the Fall.

This is a treadmill going around
No destination, around and around
The Controller abuses nature's need
To keep on feeding as we breed.

Continued…

Takes a person strong and true
To rationalize the controller's view
To transcend the conditioning of a life
To know that love is a worthy wife.

Flowering plants will seed the breeze
They have magic, not disease
Love is a lonely commitment to grow
Flowers are perfectly in love's flow.

Instinct v. Intellect

The population explosion is a direct result of our inability to learn who we are—we are as mice responding to availability.

Each succeeding doubling of population has occurred in successively shorter periods—the latest period less than 40 years (1960-1996).

Our ecosystem can no longer maintain itself. Our balancing mechanisms are schemed, ultimately, because women still give deference to natural instinct over intellect.

Women, as always, hold the key to survival.

Percolating to wholeness
Attempts to grow
Truth defined in terms we sow
Back to the baseline for another go.

'What is important?' you may ask
Procreation is important, completes the task
Keep them coming—don't even ask
Why so few reveal the mask.

Continued…

Percolating to wholeness, a brew confined
Never reaching to solve time's trial
Find the baseline, achieve the mind
Live your life safely declined.

The children grow, reflections to view
Now and then a stronger brew
Mostly though, they step in line
To pay the beast they dare not find.

Seeing no further than their feed
Building security defined by need
Continuing the recycling bleed
Ignorance has the world diseased.

The children smile and love you true
Like the mother you once knew
They reflect the best of you
You sit back and enjoy the view.

Now, you live your life declined
Expect your children to be more than you
You will push them to excel
You will guide them to your hell.

Percolating to wholeness, no gain to tell
Split personalities to make us well
Living through the seeds that swell
Truth denied, all lost in hell.

From Love we came to become the same
To find our common soulful name
To reach beyond the recycle game
To become the stillness from whence we came.

Children

Like a roar that breaks your door
Birth is trauma for the soul
Mother giving her child to hell
Cast out to be made well.

But children still remember home
All the joy and love they own
They will play and love each day
They will push your clouds away.

They won't judge or steal your pie
They have only room for joy
They will take your hand and say
'I just love you so today.'

This kind of love is pure and free
Doesn't measure any fee
It is the way that life will be
When we return to be set free.

Continued…

The tiny horns begin to grow
The child forgetting the home once known
The mind takes in the current show
Responds in kind, more things to own.

Bigger horns to push and pull
Everything is going to hell!
Going out when I should stay in
Mother always waits within.

A basic requirement for involvement is the rationalization of procreation.

All that's There

To be love, born to love
To discover that love is unaware
That no one knows the dare
To be lost in rhythm's care
Forgetting!
Forgetting!
Trying to become aware
To recover all that's there.

The Loneliness that Steals...

We need each fragile other
So that we may become another
& another!
& another!
When does it stop?
Are we just fragmented fragments of fragments
When do we become real
Who will strike the blow
Who will attack this loneliness that steals?

Recycled to View

All is here now!

Through omission, educational institutions feed the fires of deception.

Young people mostly believe that
They're brand new
Without responsibility to the past.

Nothing could be less true
Primed and suited for the future
They are the past!

Re-cycled to view
Continued anew
A chance to re-do.

Boiling the cauldron of devil stew
Stoking the fire of ancient shame
Serving the god they dare not name.

Continued…

Continuing the game
Re-cycling the pain
Never figuring the master's name.

Young people
Are carriers of the past;
A lack of ease.

Re-introduced—like bullets to a well worn gun
A crazy scheme
Things are not as they seem!

Love is Alive!

When I die
I will know that you were
My friend, my lover
My parent or perhaps even my child
Yet, we barely met
Love is alive!

Maybe you were occupied
Perhaps a nod in a crowd
A friendly gesture
A shared moment
Truth is we never leave
Love is alive!

We don't go away
We don't die—immortal!
We are forever meeting each other
Over & over & over
Meeting until we are one
Love is alive!

Continued...

Energies are interactively attractive
Seeking love
There is no time but now
The dead are alive
The alive are dead
Love is alive!

Structures are stepping stones to love
Love has no structure
All is happening now
Enjoy the dance, be aware
Awaken, awaken
Love is alive!

That nod in the crowd
Could have been your mother
Your friend, your sister
Love the chance, love the dance
Have fun, be in love
Love is alive!

Rites of Passage

To move the body towards itself
Requires a shock to make the test
A test of wills to be denied
A finer will to be defined.

The common man respects the state
Of comfort, happiness well defined
A hiding place to be most true
To living life in absence.

When man becomes a worthy disciple
He is initiated in the order of Light
He takes a test to work his truth
To open his mind, to kill the past.

The only way to find the light
Is by taking out the dark
To claim the present, to be reborn
The pain of birth to be renewed.

The loss of dark will take your heart
Will rip you up, will spit you out
Will bring your life to reaper's edge
Will make you wish that you were dead.

Continued…

But when the fury wastes its rage
A birthing process is engaged
A newborn vision will unfold
A new awareness to behold.

The grip of truth will power faith
And faith will bring the truth to bloom
A potent force to order time
The gift of life in nature's way.

Dead Man Walking

The Russian writer Fyodor Dostoyevsky rebelled against the Czar and along with others of his student group was arrested and sentenced to death. He was reprieved at the final moment.

Dostoyevsky on his way to the firing squad
Died a thousand times with each step
Drank everything in:

Each mood, each whim
Each texture, nuance, shape, color
Saw everything through the eyes of one.

Remembered!
Felt time still to outside in
All is within! All is within!

Felt eternity in a moment's thrill
Cried the tears of the damned in sin
And felt the loss he was about to win.

Sacrifice

Frustration grows as I measure the world
And realize that, as in older days
There is great need
For sacrifices to honor God
But there are no virgins prepared to die
No masses willing a noble death
The world groans in pain
Coughs & sputters, contorts & screams
She is dying
Struggling for survival
But still we will not sacrifice
To ease this suffering
We will not choose to die as the ancients did
We want it all and we want it now!

Human Folly

When the Spaniards under Cortez came upon the Aztec capital of Tenochtitlán in Mexico in 1519, they were amazed to discover a beautiful white-walled city sitting on an island in the middle of a large lake with causeways linked to it. Their astonishment soon turned to horror when they saw the vast scale of ritual sacrifices made by the Aztecs.

Ancient cultures knew intuitively that
This world is not real
Some performed ritual self-sacrifice
As a means to advantage in reality.

Continued...

They were misguided
Death to the body is an escape
Death to the mind is the sacrifice required
Body is the means to this divine advantage.

The Ancients were noble
Strong intuition without knowledge
A moth to a flame
A mother & child re-union.

In today's world
We dismiss ritual sacrifice
As savage ignorance
We replace it with a more refined ignorance.

In today's world
We believe that we are real
We believe that we have the power to create destiny;
The power to control events.

We are comfortable
Within the boundaries we can defend
We believe that this world is the real deal
And that we are it.

Whatever 'it' is?
We are not ignorant savages
Dying willingly to gain advantage
In some mythical un-provable afterlife.

We don't believe as they did
That the world is an opportunity to die well
No, we are masters of our existence
We know better.

We are sophisticated
We have information & knowledge
We can conquer space
Soon, we may bend time to our advantage.

Of course we are real!
I can pinch my skin and feel the pain
I can use my mind to create a dream
I can procreate.

Continued...

I am man becoming God
It is my birthright
My reason for being
My solemn promise.

I am man becoming God
It is my destiny to bring the human experience
To its ultimate potential—to realize itself
I am God becoming man.

To Enter the Realm

A dizzying flight
To the greatest height
To capture fear
The enemy of love.

But what is love?
Love is eternal life
Has no point of reference
Timeless.

Being fearless
Is to be more than brave
Not a passing phase
An insight.

Continued…

An attitude of death
It must invest
A rite of passage
A shift.

The abyss looms
The final doom
A sacred chance
To heal.

To enter the realm
Rising above the plundered shells
Hear their screaming tortured yells
And know that they don't hear themselves

A Kingdom for a Horse

Elizabeth Woodville accuses Richard Plantagenet of murdering her children in order to gain the throne of England.

A horse! A horse!
My kingdom for a horse
Tragic bargain
Richard lives.

Continued…

To be so reduced from one's truth
As to be unavailable for comment
Lost in delusion
Morally bankrupt.

To have sought
And to have conquered the kingdom
Over the blood of innocents
Only to find that the fruit did not match the promise.

To cling so desperately
As to barter everything for a reprieve
Tragic illusion that life is real
Still slicing the air with his sword of steel.

Every life is measured by its need
Everything is perfect all the time
All designed to make us real
Each moment a forgiving scream.

Nest Pest

Family structures, if they do not honor their children as do the birds in Spring have as much utility as stagnant pools in a river of change. The shock of being pushed out of the nest is an initiation into self-awareness. It is a rite of passage that initiates the young to the death process which is the only path to life (completeness).

Liberties taken, tempers flare
Need to cut loose on my cares
Need a safe place to vent the pain
Trusting your love I abuse your care.

All the passions of my past
Demand expression, won't depart
All those things left unresolved
All my issues just won't dissolve.

Feel like a funnel unable to flow
Pressure building, want to blow!
But I am blocked—don't know how to go
No one taught me about the flow.

Continued…

Frustration builds and so it goes
Many mistakes—attempts to grow
Like a prisoner with a million keys
Wish I knew the one that frees.

Maybe I am being a pest
Want security without the fee
But, they won't do what birds know best
Too afraid I'll fail the test.

Angel Light

'Guide them like a flower in shock for they hold the key to freedom's lock.'

'I must tell you about my plight
About confusion, rage and fright
About how my body changed your mind
Made me feel a lesser kind.

'I was just a girl of twelve
On my bike—a boy of nerve
I was very much with you
Boys and girls all fit one shoe.

'But when my body made me she
I found out the world was 'he'
I became a sight to see
He became the force to be.

'When my blood of shame was free
I became the best of me:
A flower's peak of bursting growth
Spiting the conspirator's mortal yoke.

Continued…

'Thought I was quite out of mind
Felt so strong this urge to bind
Want to mate, I need my kind
I want the love I left behind.

'How I suffered for this instinct raid
This world's a patriarchal fade
Much forgotten, much is gone
I was used—became confused.

'Killed my child, my gentle way
Used my body, sex to play
Tried so hard to build love's way
But only love more with each day.

'Now I have a fear-bound mind
Abortions made me change and say
I will measure how I play
I will play my cards to stay.

'My fragile heart I keep at bay
Measuring my love to control my pay
No one prepared me—I hate this!!
Killing love is the price to pay.'

When the Angel flowers to light
The girl has wisdom to ease our fright
A special time, a glorious find
Human potential beyond the mind.

A rite of passage must be found
To reap this harvest, plant new ground
To nurture this most precious gift
To teach the girl the quantum shift.

Nature is a garden of remembrance
Inspired perfection's teasing dance
All humanity is perfect too
Wisdom comes when flowers are true.

Suicide

'Crossing over I felt a breeze, a gentle tempting seductive tease. An invite to become undone, a chance to live as few have done.'

Quietly I sit drinking my beer
Young man asked
'Are you from Ireland?'
We talk of druids & ancient lore
Said he was a poet.

Found him wise
Of ageless truth
Said he was distracted, came from the hospital;
Girlfriend tried to commit suicide
Wanted to leave the world.

A year since, raped
Lost her job
Depressed & stressed
An angel of light like a beacon at night
Attracting the darkness.

The darkness came and took the light
A moment's reprieve in a sea of loss
To ease the pain at such a cost
But nothing stolen can kill the pain
Only balance can ease the shame.

Continued…

The light was taken for a moment's reprieve
Leaving an angel with broken wings
No longer to be warmed by the breath of innocence
No longer to fly on the wings of hope
No longer to live the immortal death of nature.

It is a trap most cruel
To protect is the rule
To build a tower
To save a fool
The sword will rule!

Spirits soar as freedom rules
But when the attacks come
They begin to 'think'
Knowing reduces to measure fear
A steel trap descends.

Now owned by fear
Control is the Seer
Subtle traps for the wise & clear
Whispering, whispering in their ear
Measuring all they have to fear.

To clear the air one must die on cue
Become as dead
Living in the spirit world
Coming here to work & play
Nothing is real!

Learn to laugh at control
Tell it you're already dead
Diffuse its influence
It can rape your flower
For this is not your power.

Transfer your center
From here to there
Remember, you died!
You committed suicide
No longer alive.

Now you are free
Powerful, alive & free
Immortal—enjoy!
Nothing to do
Just be.

Cannon Fodder

We do not know the master we serve. We must come to understand why we repeatedly cripple ourselves and then make our children pay the price.

Handsome young men
Blue-eyed sons
Ripped the child from mother's breast
Sent them to the shower of death.

Horror after horror did they invest
These blue-eyed sons of Aryan 'best'
Weaned from a cradle of ignorance and fear
Even the Jew has fed these tears.

History repeats—over and over
Building momentum to become undone
How can we save our innocent sons
From becoming fodder for the conspirator's gun?

Continued…

202 | Thomas F. Kitt

Many things our children become
Reflect the messages of distorted views
Views the demon needs to use
To create momentum or its life to lose.

Following blindly, doing as they're told
Safe and secure—validation molds
They will jump when fear shoots the floor
They will march to even the score.

Always ready—march at dawn
Noble Knight to be re-born
Feed their fears, design their hate
Fire the guns to satiate.

Who is to blame, you might ask
'Not I, my children are the best
All have passed their scholars' tests
They have values—religion's best!'

Conventional standards are a trap
Truth gets lost in reaction's sap
Religious containment's—attempts to One
Bigger boxes to divide the sun.

Random procreation is a crying shame
Children teaching us what to gain
Ending up feeding the conspirator's game
Forgetting what they came to claim.

Our ignorance, fear and ego to blame
Procreation—our means to neutralize this hell
But we abuse this wisdom well
Will not let the flower excel.

Responsibility must be taken for their wisdom to remain
Beyond the portals crying stocks
Guide them like a flower in shock
For they hold the key to freedom's lock.

'Love thy neighbor as thyself'
Children have this special glow
A message beyond the mind to know
Unify and be like snow.

Male Bonding

I said to my 19-year-old son
After he tells me about this 'hot girl' he met
'Wow! 22
You should call her.

Just think of all she can teach you
Likely sexually active
May be hot for you
Probably sees you as a stud.'

He looks at me unsure
Shy & gentle soul
Just trying to find his way
I felt ashamed.

Damage done
Fell into my own trap
Became what I hate!
Why did I do that?

Giving in to insecurity & shame
Trying to justify my own gluttonous violations
Honoring the Cyclops
By sacrificing my own child to the fire.

Continued…

I want him to be more than me
To expand my awareness
Why didn't I tell him what I know
Allow him to follow his own heart.

Tell him that we are a oneness
Fractured into loneliness
That women & men are broken pieces
That body is a vehicle to soul.

I should have told him that soul has no sex
That animal nature must be transcended
I should have told him that life is about unity
A journey home.

The availability of sex makes it a plaything
But sex is not a plaything
Sex is a sacrament
A means to honor love.

I should have told him that love has no master
And that all he need be concerned about
Is his capacity to love for love's sake
Sex will find its place.

Love & sex are synonymous
But if they are divided by animal need
Then all is reduced to an addict's sense of loss
Stealing heaven at such a cost.

Next time around I may be wiser—maybe not?
Wisdom gets caught in the webs of time
And when moments are not aware
The beast will free the snare.

Love is not about sex but sex should always be about love.

Young Man

I am a young man strong and true
Have no clue of what to do
They tell me things that are not true
Fill the pints to clear my view.

I can't measure what is true
Just repeating what is done
Patterns of patterns
Chase the carrot is all I do.

And if I should catch this carrot
The world will seem untrue
No definition, nothing to view
Again, to begin anew.

Endless, endless, chasing games
Some with longer times to fail
Sometimes lifetimes chasing tails
Mindless, worthless, useless games.

Continued…

I am a young man strong and true
Only want the proper view
Everyone with a lock and key
Maybe they want to steal what's free?

Maybe they really don't have a clue
Just chasing what defines their view
Who is to blame for this chasing game?
Something sinister that needs a name.

Half Mast

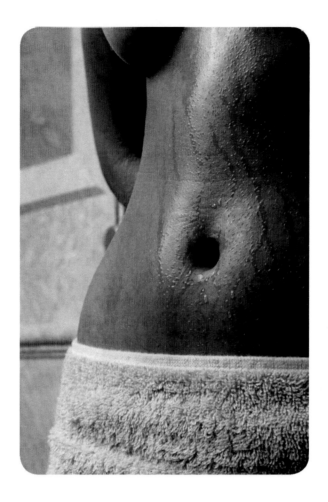

Nudist resort, young woman
She is shy, wears a towel
Sunning with her parents
Cell phone rings
She moves away for privacy
Overheard by elderly man
Uses the information to hold her in conversation
She: polite, innocent, naïve
He at half-mast
Talked of psychology, philosophy
& college things
His thrill was her violation
While I admired his practiced skill
In containing the prey
I hated him deeply for his deception
My deception!

Continued…

Maybe he touched a chord?
Parents came to rescue
But still the professor rattled on
As if to completely diffuse
As if the parents did not know
As if in normal flow
The mast now down to show.

Abuse

Dusk!
Nine-year-old girl outside a bar
Waiting alone.

Absently crawls onto the hood of the car
Curls up, large soda
Stays a few moments—bored!

Climbs a nearby stairs
Wants to play
But no kids around.

Walks around
Notices me
Senses danger—primal alert!

'When will my daddy take me home?
Scared…
School tomorrow—homework!'

Rain Forest

Indigenous peoples forced to fight
To remain in balance with the land
Their ancient ways in compromise
Their spiritual truth in the mist it hides.

They come with machines
And righteous dreams
No direction except to eat
The noble savage in defeat.

Plunder the land
Pollute the water
Extract the metals
Breed and settle.

The indigenous peoples
Through courage and pain
Must compromise to remain
Temporary relief in a sea of shame.

Continued…

But the damage is done
Nothing's been won
Minds on the run
Sucked into the gun.

This is our world in decay
Our dying display
Procreative irresponsibility
Devouring our children like cannibals to stay.

Fringe Dwellers

We are the fringe dwellers.

Outside the flow
A mainstream tangent
Separate & alone
Existing in stagnant pools
Isolated in dull awareness of something lost
The sense of being apart, removed
The fringe dwellers organize within linear patterns
Ravaging, devouring, destroying to survive
Developing negative momentum
Survival of the fittest!
Justifying actions by democratic validation:
Common denominator plunging in ignorance
As pearls of wisdom get lost in walls
'Increase & multiply'
On and on it continues

Continued…

A beast out of control
Or, is it out of control?
As we remain content to hunt for fleas on the animal's back
The beast is galloping to extinction
The beast doesn't mind—our ignorance at play
The driver doesn't mind
He's making a deposit at the bank
Everyone happy
Love those fleas.

The Pain I Am

'Evil lives through how we think
Validation seeds the genocidal womb
The surface bubble a Fascist hell
Baby Adolph to make us well.'

I am the Jew that lived the slaughter
With a view so true, I am so real
My past was slaughtered in the pain
The view I feel is yours to see.

I am the man who felt the futility
Of seeing innocence die in pain
The master race was theirs to have
The price to pay was innocence betrayed.

I am assaulted by the thought
That I am saved to tell the tale
Of pain so cruel it has no peer
Perpetrated by all as one sad seer.

Continued…

The Huns came and slaughtered all
The kings of England slaughtered more
The eastern nomad took his toll
The wars of Asia bested all.

But none can best the beast being born
Of modern hearts still in shame
We blame Hitler
But Hitler was just one of us.

We dare to think that we are free
To cast the blame in Hitler's way
He was a man as you & I
He was the invention of our thoughts.

We are a world in God's disgrace
We choose the leaders of our race
To serve the thinking we formulate
We move away when they disgrace.

What has changed? Nothing, I say
The book has passed to save the day
The evil will is only saved
By giving blame to local demand.

Evil lives through how we think
Validation seeds the genocidal womb
The surface bubble a Fascist hell
Baby Adolph to make us well.

Genocide

World of pain! World of sorrow!
Their terror enjoyed by evil's spawn
Give a thought to what occurred
And cry the cry of killer pain.

They became a vent to ease the load
A way for God to take the reins
A means to change the worldly view
That might is right and God is dead.

It is a repeating theme
A primordial scream
A whore to a virgin true
A twisted point of view.

They were the best of cultured man
They earned their advantages by honest means
The wasteful saw the view
That Jews were trying to steal their homes.

They became a race with ego-pride
They were the best at ordering time
They made a pact with Satan's friend
And gave their souls to ego-pride.

Continued…

Satan came from a meter grave
He is a meter in his frame
He is a demon in man's place
His name was Hitler, our disgrace.

He took the fear and made a deal
He said that they were men of destiny
A force to purge the world of greed
An Aryan cleanse all bright & pure.

He mixed a brew of terror & fear
Fed them 'till their fire was fueled
Unleashed on all he deemed untrue
Cutting, cutting to be brand new.

Evil has its power by fear
But good is all alone
Seduced by fear they bellied bare
Few were left where hero's dare.

Demons raged through dying screams
Their wanton slaughter became a drug
The more the blood, the more the thirst
They feasted fear, gave the devil his due.

The victims were taken to their graves
To shallow pits with lime to waste
To ovens fit for fiery hell
To chambers gassed with chlorine's ghost.

They were denied their right to live
They were the lucky ones
The others suffered the pain of experimentation
Guinea pigs to serve the Reich.

Human life a thing to waste
Experiments to build the master race
Humanity in its worst disgrace
A horror so profound!

The mass of evil has the power
To fortify the smallest sin
To give it force beyond its life
To subjugate the Intellectual mind.

Continued…

Beware your thoughts of being secure
They will plant you in Satan's grave
Feed you with your worldly wiles
Lock you in to make you fierce.

Will turn you loose when Master comes
To find the view that wrong is right
Will fight to serve the Master's whim
Truth is dead! God is dead!

All thinking is movement of evil
Thoughtful, sly & in control
Beware this beast of your disgrace
Lest your Hitler find your face.

Genocide, a tragic and saving disgrace.

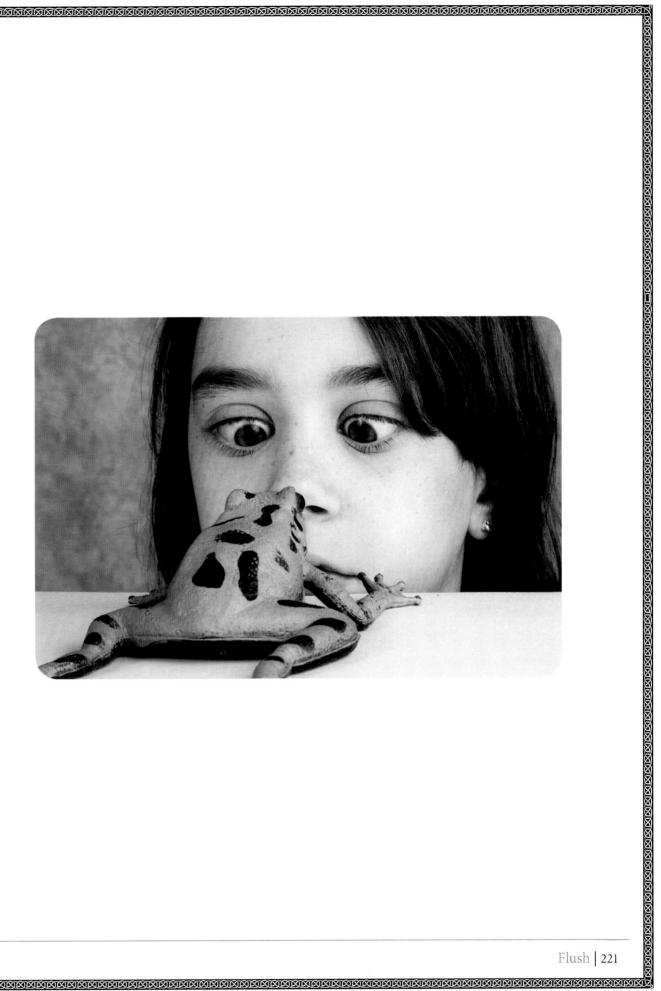

Inching towards Liberation

'Thinking' is what I am
A reflection of truth
Outside myself
Barreling through space & time
Out of control, lost!
I am seeking to know—what?
I am lost
Groping desperately
For the strands of interconnection
Trying to figure it out?
This pain, this loss
I'm inching my way toward death
Towards freedom
I am inching towards liberation.

A Conductor moves his baton
Above a mesh of sea-like waves
But, they're not as waves—
No rolling constant wake
More like isolated crests and falls
All connected, all the same—but different too!
A symphony of movement
Groaning, straining, sometimes sparkling
Always moving—dancing!
I saw this view from a place beyond
Beyond the themes of time
Beyond the worlds.

Reality and Illusion

Everything in the universe is movement and thereby illusion. When we learn who we are we become Magician's and play with the illusions.

There is no middle ground with reality:
Things are either real, or not!

If nothing is real
Then all is illusion.

If all is illusion
Then all is magical.

If all is magical
Then everything is possible.

If everything is possible
Then we have no limitations.

If we have no limitations
Then we are capable of becoming real.

Pixie

When we stop trying to control we become magical.

Cooperation is the key to magic.

A Pixie came so pure & true
Tried to catch it to give it feel
Tried to trap it to make it real.

Tried to own it so I may feel
All the things I need to heal
But it went away—this wisping thing.

Heard its flutter of pixie wings
Felt a sting deep down within
Knew I had a ways to win.

Because children sometimes claim to see faeries
Doesn't mean that the faeries are not real
Of course they're real!

As real as you and I
They have texture and depth
Can talk and play and even cry.

They are illusions
Thinking forms brought to existence
By thought process.

Children have no expectations
No blocks—they are available;
At one with themselves and their possibilities.

Continued…

Just as you and I, they are limitless
They imagine and they believe
In the goodness of things.

Nature cannot but respond
For nature is our love in action
Responding in perfection to every demand.

The dance of the faeries
The little people
Are figments of imagination.

Natural responses
Wisping, beautiful manifestations of love,
Available only to the pure of heart.

Faeries—just as all material things
Have no permanent reality;
Cannot exist alone.

Their wisping existence
Comes to form only by the momentum
Of the child's imagination.

From faeries to war
This is the way of everything
The way of nature.

In the universe:
All repeats the same; all is healing;
All is illusion; all is magical—all is possible.

Fairytale

Told me they're her playmates
Independent personalities
Insisting on their own agendas
That sometimes they even sneak up behind her
And nudge her for attention
She said that
Her own plans were usually put on hold
As she got older
They gradually lost their outer manifestations
Transferring to the inner experience of her mind.
She said that
They were growing up with her
Later she commented that
It was probably her own removal from
The aware-less world to the aware
That caused them to disappear & hide.

Continued…

Now a young woman
No longer are her playmates available
But she still remembers
Knows that when this time of reconciliation is past
She will once again return
Where again her friends will come out to play
And the Kingdom will open at her command.

Imagine!

Imagine!

Love without end
No body to defend
Nothing to offend.

Imagine!

No need to eat
No cause for greed
No cars, no houses, no phones.

Imagine!

No hurt, nothing to alert
No wars, no fear, no disease
Everywhere at once it seems.

Imagine!

No me, no you
No trees, no animals
No births, no death.

Continued…

Imagine!

No separation for us to see
No beginning to reach an end
Peace.

Imagine!

No body to offend
Nothing to defend
Love without end.

Imagine!

Moving Feast

The world is a moving feast
The only constant:
Change!
Enjoy the feast.

Skirts all aflare
She moved through the fair
A Will o' the Wisp
Magic in the air.

A bird in spring
Doing its bird thing
Complete and true
All things new.

A mother's care
As the babies dare
No ego scares
A dive through the air.

Moment to moment is a portal
For the ancients to come alive
Time is a series from a rapid frame
Stop a moment and heaven is gained.

Flower

Life's as simple as can be
Watch a flower
It will show you how to be
Letting go to be set free
Life's as simple as can be.

Constant death is a birthing wheel.

Sacred Wind

Like a feather in the wind
I will always move and bend
I will see each move you dare
As a prayer for my care.

I will not expect a thing
I will live with what you bring
I will move with each new wind
I will settle if and when.

I have felt this sacred wind
Pushing me to please transcend
I have felt this hunting wind
I have known the truth it brings.

Decide!

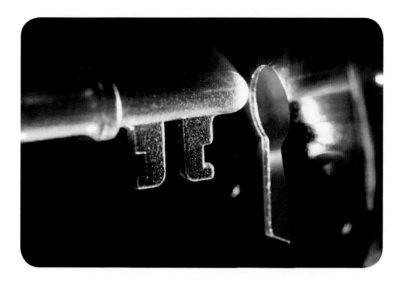

'Leave your things and follow'
An invite to release from worry
To live under love's protection
To become undone.

Decide!

No more fear
No financial problems
No problems of any kind
Everything perfect all the time.

Decide!

Genuine effort can not but reward
There is no outside authority
For we are our own initiator & judge
Individually & collectively we are God.

Decide!

All being One must be accepted or not!
Choose it or lose it
Choose heaven or hell
Given a mansion don't live in the outhouse.

Decide!

Afraid

I am living for love to free
To sail the winds of endless sea
I exist within love's dare
Afraid my needs will be its slayer.

Of human touch I am afraid to know
So afraid to upset the flow
Afraid you'll dim this kindling glow
Afraid you'll want to run the show.

Need to love you, to feel your care
But afraid you'll trap me in your fear
I see evil lurking there
Know my Achilles' heel is bare.

So, should you enter my circle of fire
Please be naked in love's care
Trust that love is not a snare
Total security for those who dare.

Measure me from whence we came
Know that life is love inflamed
No more worries, all is same
Matter is love's whoring dame.

Death

Socrates knew the truth and used his death creatively to show us that we are immortal.

Death is coming home to your own
A way to breach the mortal hold
A way to let the truth unfold
A way to see that love is whole.

Death is where your love was born
Where you remember what you have scorned
Where you knew what you must do
Where you saw what you just blew.

Returning to view, forgetting anew
Death is a bridge from hell to you
Crossing over, your finest mile
If you continue the same shoe size.

Continued…

The gift is found when you devise
That you have died—yet still alive
You will reach to touch your soul
You will remember the love you own.

The greatest joy in life is death
The mind is forced to acquiesce
Opens one to know the soul
To know true joy is mind disowned.

Constant death should one invest
In overcoming the obstacles of life's test
Plato said so as he died
Socrates lived death   Hemlock lies.

The realized archetype of humanity is immortality.

Really Wise

The woman is attempting to remove herself from the desires of the men. She knows that one is all and all is love. There is no 'one' in life, only separation, need and strife.

Are you really wise
Do you live to die
Do you measure every moment
As your last.

Do you play your cards
Hedge your bets
Are you alive and well
In the throes of hell.

Are you on the edge
Of love to pledge
Lock and key
A place to shell.

Continued…

Do you know the prize
Are you naked
Are you sharp and clear
Each moment to disappear.

Like a river to fear
Are you really clear
Do you live out there—
Somewhere out there!

Have you lost your mind
Are your names undone
Do you have no other
Do you die to live.

Are you really wise?

Odyssey

Live! Live to love this beauteous death
Invite the Ancients to the feast
Sit them down to spin their tales
Man the oars and set the sail.

Travel to all the ports of call
Seek awareness about the fall
Learn to master the trials and scorn
Fall apart to be reborn.

I am with you—close and clear
Forever whispering in your ear
Helping you view those honeyed thorns
As tranquil beauty marred by storms.

Allow the sail seek what it will
Man is nothing against this wind
This sacred seeking wind that bends
Forever guiding to transcend.

The journey's end is pure and still
No more sail filled with wind
No more aching to defend
No more time to die in sin.

Possibility for Flight

Catholics & Protestants
Moslems & Christians
Jews & everyone else
Man & woman
Black & white
Salt & pepper
East & West
Yin & yang
Up & down
In & out

All are birds in flight to the heart of truth
But not all birds are capable of flight
So beware the turkey you create
Never attack the balancing wing
For therein lies the possibility for flight.

The Bell Tolls

Destruction is in the air
Change is imperative
No longer can we revel in the bliss of ignorance
The conditioning of education
The misrepresentations nurtured by traditions of fear
Preparing us like perfect firewood
Time to wake up!
We are dying
Being used up like a food supply
Continuing to defer our obligations to our children
Conditioning them to do the same
Bartering our denial as the well goes dry
Choosing to misunderstand the work
The work is to unify not multiply
By giving in to the beast of loneliness;
Our pervasive fear
We submit to a control unknown
By refusing to rationalize this force
We guarantee its future
We are dying!
Like hollow logs empty in our abundance
By our denial
We have cannibalized our very soul
Compromised our mother earth
The monster is feeding in our garden
The bell is tolling
But we are oblivious.

Angel of Death

We are constantly and completely Love and nothing less. When we come to energy (life) we become less than we are. As we scramble for identity we chase ourselves through the pain we create until the very force of it awakens us to our loss.

I carry a sword in one hand
And I carry death in the other.

I am here to create bedlam
I am fierce & relentless.

Nothing is safe from me
I am sharp & clear.

Continued…

I am dangerous
I will cut deep & true.

And the blood will flow like a river
But still I will cut & cleave.

And they will scream in agony
I will hear but still I will cut.

I will cut until they are all dead!
And we shall begin anew.

And I will sharpen my sword
And I will watch & watch.

For I am the protector of life
I am the angel of death.

The pain of our loss is such that there is nothing we will not do to gain it back.

Peace

When we know who we are we will become peaceful.

Peace is not the absence of war
The calm before the storm
Or passions spent on nature's call
True peace has no rhythm
No enmity to recall
True peace is the personal knowledge
That each and every one is all.

The Thing to Win

In truth there is no death.

Natural rhythm is not ours to win

We are not trees
Or flowers
Or birds of wing.

We are lost in nature's thing
We are God
We are not a thing.

Divine Living

Life is a perfect orchestration of love.

Perfect, perfect, always perfect

Be aware you are divine
You order pain to show the way
Heaven is a moment everlasting and whole
Pain is love showing us home
Perfect, perfect, always perfect.

Release your bondage and acquiesce
Become a creature of the dance
A passenger on a ride
Rise and fall
Perfect, perfect, always perfect.

Don't disturb the Maestro's gift
Move in harmony's wake
Be perfection in your moments
Love is all
Perfect, perfect, always perfect.

Continued…

Enter the rhythm of the dance
Mine is yours, yours is mine
Relax in the peace of knowing
You are shadow to yourself
Perfect, perfect, always perfect.

Know this truth
Relax!
Allow your rhythm find its tone
No limitations, no fear
Perfect, perfect, always perfect.

www.onepositive.com